Our Texas Heritage

Ethnic Traditions and Recipes

by

Dorothy McConachie

Republic of Texas Press

Library of Congress Cataloging-in-Publication Data

McConachie, Dorothy.
  Our Texas heritage: ethnic traditions and recipes / Dorothy McConachie.
    p. cm.
  ISBN 1-55622-785-X
  1. Ethnology--Texas. 2. Texas--ethnic relations. 3. Texas--Social life and
  customs. 4. Cookery--Texas. I. Title.

  F395.A1 M39 2000
  305.8'009764--dc21
                                 00-030387
                                   CIP

Printed in the United States of America

ISBN 1-55622-785-X
10 9 8 7 6 5 4 3 2
0006

All inquiries for volume purchases of this book should be addressed to Wordware Publishing, Inc., at 2320 Los Rios Boulevard, Plano, Texas 75074. Telephone inquiries may be made by calling:
(972) 423-0090

Contents

Preface

About the Recipes...

When I was a little girl helping my mother make the wonderful pastries and delicious treats of her childhood, we used my grandmother's recipes. But we did not use exactly the same techniques my grandmother had used as a young bride on the Texas prairie. We used an electric mixer and electric stove. We chilled the dough and saved leftovers in a refrigerator or freezer (called a deep freeze back then) rather than in an icebox. The old way was too much work. Plus the results from using the current technology were more uniform.

Since the days of my childhood, technology has transformed the kitchen even more. Today we have microwaves and dishwashers. We can go to our neighborhood grocery to buy chopped onion and celery, or we can chop our own without tears in a food processor. The recipes from my grandmother's era do not reflect the changing kitchen.

An example of this is the recipe for Danish apple cake that appears on page 164. The original recipe that my grandmother used calls for fresh apples that need to be peeled and cooked. A later version of the same recipe uses dried apples that only needed to be cooked. Because it is now possible to buy good applesauce, the recipe in this book calls for that. My grandmother used dried breadcrumbs baked in the oven with brown sugar and cinnamon. I use graham cracker crumbs that I either purchase or crush in a food processor. It does not matter; the end result is just as delicious.

To my way of thinking, there is no virtue in slaving over a hot, wood-burning stove to make traditional ethnic food. Grandmother had no choice; she had to spend hours preparing meals for her family. Today we have choices. We also have jobs, carpools, volunteer commitments, and hundreds of other things to do with our time. When we want to taste the foods of our heritage, we do not want to spend hours in the kitchen. By updating the preparation techniques in traditional recipes, it is possible to get virtually the same results with a lot less work and a lot less time.

The recipes in this book largely come from first- and second-generation Americans who remember how their mothers and grandmothers cooked. They have continued preparing these dishes in much the same way. I have tried to simplify these recipes so busy cooks today can enjoy the wonderful tastes of the past.

Lard was commonly used for frying and in baking. It was available and the results were wonderful, flaky biscuits and pastries. Today we have choices that are healthier for our bodies. Instead of lard, recipes in this book call for shortening, cooking oil, butter, or margarine. In most cases the option is yours—use your favorite brand or type of shortening or oil. Usually when butter is listed, margarine is given as an alternative. Do not use a soft, whipped, or "diet" margarine. These have too much air or water in them to give the best results. Instead, you may use regular stick margarine. I personally do not like the "butter flavored" margarines—I think they taste more like artificial butter flavor than real butter. But if you prefer this type, go ahead and use it.

In the past, pans had to be greased before the batter or dough was baked. The nonstick cooking sprays are a quick, easy, and calorie-saving way to keep foods from burning on the pan and to help make cleaning easier. The baking sprays that combine oil and flour are ideal for spraying cake pans.

Many people today are afraid of using yeast. To them the word "yeast" in a recipe means lots of work and time. This is no longer true if you use the rapid rise yeast that requires only one rising. A rest period of ten minutes substitutes for the first rising. This saves a lot of time and makes working with yeast so much easier. The directions for using this type of yeast are a little different from the traditional yeast. Fortunately, these differences make it much harder to "kill" the yeast and end up with heavy, flat bread. The yeast recipes in this collection have been written to take advantage of the one-rise method.

All yeast breads as well as a few others still require kneading. I personally like the process of kneading because I like the way the dough feels on my hands. When my children were little, they would knead the dough for hours if I would let them and I rarely got a chance to knead. If you do not have young children or do not like to knead, use your food processor or a bread hook on your mixer. Either way, you will get great results with a lot less work.

During the pioneer days of Texas the settlers used a lot of salt to increase the palatability of their food. With the warnings we get today about consuming too much salt, I have decreased the amount of salt used in most recipes. Use your own palate as a guide.

The people who came to Texas found an abundance of pecan trees. Almost every group used nuts somewhere in their cooking. However, the nut used in the old country was usually something that was available where they came from. Since the pecan was so plentiful here, they substituted it in their recipes. If you prefer a different type of nut or find a better price on some other kind than the one listed in the recipe, go ahead and try it. Our thrifty forefathers (and mothers) would have approved.

Whenever a recipe calls for something to be chopped, diced, or sliced, use whatever method you prefer. A food processor works fine, but so does a paring knife. Unfortunately, I have not discovered an easy way to peel raw potatoes, yet. The early settlers tried to invent gadgets to peel potatoes and apples, but none were successful enough to make it to the twenty-first century. And I always melt butter or margarine in the microwave.

Once upon a time everyone got milk from the cow in the barn. The milk from the cow came with a built-in supply of cream. Cooks used this cream to make wonderfully rich desserts, custards, and other delicious treats. A recipe that requires cream means an extra trip to the grocery store for me because my carton of milk does not come with a built-in cream supply. Where milk is given as an option, the results may not be quite as rich, but they will be good. Since I do not churn my own butter, I do not have a ready supply of buttermilk, either. The powdered variety works just as well; plus, it has a longer shelf life.

I chose the recipes in this book based on several criteria. Some of the recipes are for familiar foods that we associate with a particular ethnic group. Others are special recipes for special occasions celebrated by the ethnic group. And still others are recipes that may be unfamiliar to outsiders but are common to that particular ethnic group. Some groups have an intertwined heritage—the Polish and the Ukrainians and the Wends and the Germans, for example. Many of their traditional recipes are very similar. I have tried not to duplicate recipes except for when the name may be the same but the taste is different. This makes for an interesting comparison of how different groups took the same basic ingredients, made the same recipe, but added their own individual touch.

I tried to include at least one easy recipe from each group that a student of Texas history could make and take to school for the class to sample. Knowing the food of a culture helps us to understand the people. Of course, each ethnic group has many more wonderful recipes that do not appear in this book. And each recipe has as many variations as there are cooks. So whenever you try any of these recipes, feel free to adapt or change anything you want. That is exactly what the cooks of times past did, and that is why we so fondly remember their meals.

My intent has been to maintain the original ethnic qualities of the foods in this book. At the same time, I have also attempted to simplify the recipes as much as possible without ruining the ethnic quality of the food. Now real people can prepare and enjoy the foods brought to our state by the courageous people who came before us.

Acknowledgements

So many people deserve a big hug for their help with this book. For every culture there were kind people who spent considerable time with me, talking about the traditions of their childhoods and how they still uphold these traditions, their recipes, and their festivals. Some of these people are:

Greg Howard, Marvin Johnson, Evelyn Kasper, Myrtle Waldman, Don Barkett, Louise Raggio, Virgina Concho, Elin Greenberg, Rosalie Rodrigues, Susan Hempfelt, Diane McCartney, Phyllis Wells, Ukrainian American Society, Italian American Club, Irish American Society, Danish Heritage Society, St. Peter the Apostle Catholic Church in Dallas, Beverly Burmeier, Jenny Davis, and especially, Ginnie Bivona.

Also, I would like to thank my family for being such good sports as I experimented with these recipes from so many different cultures.

Introduction

When the food of a culture survives, the culture itself continues. *Our Texas Heritage: Ethnic Traditions and Recipes* is a book that celebrates the cultures as well as the cuisine of the various groups that make up Texas. The first outsiders who arrived at the Texas shores found that this vast area was already populated by groups of indigenous people who greeted them with friendliness and kindness. These tribes used the greeting "Tejas," or friends, thus introducing the name for the land that would become our state.

The Spanish came first, looking for riches and souls to convert to Christianity. They were most successful in the area that became Mexico because that is where their rule lasted the longest. After the Mexicans gained their freedom from Spanish rule, they realized that to maintain their control over Texas, they needed to colonize the area. Efforts to do this with native Mexicans failed. Mexico lifted the ban on colonization by foreigners when it granted Stephen F. Austin permission to bring settlers from the United States. Enterprising individuals from other countries petitioned the Mexican government to establish colonies in Texas.

Conditions in Europe were ripe for enticing colonists to leave their homes and venture to a new land. Laws changed, freeing peasants from the land. Though no longer bound to the land, their prospects still remained limited. In addition, wars, famine, depressed economies, and widespread discrimination made life hard. Rumors and reports from the adventurous few who had already crossed the ocean enticed others to follow.

The United States, especially after our Civil War, seemed like a land of limitless opportunity. Many left the hardships of Europe to seek their fortunes by sailing to New York. The climate there matched that in Northern Europe, and the route across the Atlantic was the most direct. To encourage people to make the longer journey to Texas, land agents spread the word about the wondrous advantages of coming here.

The greatest pull was the prospect of owning large tracts of their own land, an impossible dream for peasants in Europe. Texas was also a land where persecuted groups could practice their religions and preserve their heritage, language, and culture without governmental influence.

During the eighteen hundreds and especially during the last half of that century, immigrants from all over the world came to Texas. Whatever unknown hardships awaited them seemed preferable to the certainty of poverty, hunger, and often persecution in the old country. These brave pioneers brought with them little more than a few tools and basic necessities. But they carried within themselves the rich traditions of their native land that bound them together as unique groups.

The events and celebrations of the old home traveled across the ocean to give comfort and a sense of belonging to the newcomers in this strange land. At every gathering, be it a religious or social celebration or an ordinary family dinner, the tastes and smells of familiar foods from their former lives in a land far away eased their transition into being Americans.

Within a few generations, most assimilated into the American melting pot. Communities that were originally settled by immigrants from one country or area welcomed others into their midst. Young people left the close-knit nest to pursue their education and careers. Intermarriage and Americanization diluted the influence of ethnic cultures; however, the stories, traditions, and foods from the early years are preserved today by the children of the brave immigrants and their grandchildren and great-grandchildren, who are now searching for their own heritage.

Our Texas Heritage celebrates the cultural and culinary history of various ethnic groups that came and settled in Texas. Each group has its own unique story that contributes to the rich heritage of all of us. I chose to limit the scope of this book to those fourteen groups who came roughly between the Civil War and World War I because they give a good sampling of the various beliefs, celebrations, and foods the colonists brought.

Before grocery stores were only a short drive away from everyone's home, cooks (usually the women) used whatever was available to prepare their comfort foods as well as the ceremonial dishes of their culture. When their favorite recipe ingredients were not available, they had to improvise with new ones. Few of the recipes were written, but were rather passed down from mother to daughter or from friend to friend. Even then there were as many variations of a traditional dish as there were cooks. So if you want to adapt any recipe to better suit your family's tastes, go ahead. Our forebears would have approved!

The First Ones Here—

Native Americans in Texas

Tuesday night is Cherokee night. No one dresses in feathers and beads. No one beats a tom-tom or dances to its rhythm. Instead this is the night Greg Howard, a Cherokee himself, teaches the Cherokee language. Some of the people who come to his classes are Cherokee, others belong to different Native American tribes, and still others are not Indian at all—just interested. Regardless of their background, most people who come to his classes are in for a surprise. They come expecting to learn a few words and a little bit about the Cherokee culture. What they do not expect to learn is that the Cherokee language is also a written language with its own alphabet and spellings. In fact, in the eighteen hundreds there were several Cherokee language newspapers in publication.

The Cherokees came from a vast area that included what is now part of Tennessee, Georgia, the Carolinas, Virginia, and Alabama. They were primarily civilized farmers who cultivated corn, beans, and various types of squash before the Europeans arrived. But they also hunted and gathered wild plants for food and medicines. They were a peaceful people who maintained good relations with the first Europeans and other tribes. At least they did until the American settlers began moving west and encroaching on their territory.

Those Cherokees who tired of fighting the westward-moving European settlers followed Chief Duwali to an area that is now Arkansas. This group became known as the Western branch of the Cherokees, and they were the ones who moved into Texas in the first quarter of the nineteenth century.

This was a critical point in Texas history. Within a short period of time Texas won its freedom from Mexico, became an independent nation, joined the United States, and then seceded with the Confederacy. In all of these revolutions, both sides of the conflict wanted the Cherokees and the other Indian nations to take sides with them. The Cherokees wisely declined and remained neutral.

When Sam Houston (an adopted Cherokee) was president of the Republic of Texas, he negotiated a fair treaty with the Cherokees, but the Senate never ratified it. Mirabu Lamar then succeeded Houston as president of the Republic. He wanted the Indian lands for American settlers so he disregarded Houston's treaty. In protest, Chief Duwali led a revolt that resulted in the Texas Cherokees being moved to Indian Territory in what is now Oklahoma. Here they were reunited with the Eastern branch of the Cherokees. The Eastern Cherokees where among those Indians marched from Georgia along what is now known as "The Trail of Tears." The name is derived from the large numbers, mainly women and children, who died along the way.

The Apaches are another Native American group that, in an attempt to preserve their heritage, left their mark on Texas. Like the Cherokees, they migrated west and then south whenever settlers taking their land displaced them. They also lived close to nature, hunting and gathering only what they needed. Unlike the Cherokees, however, the Apaches were a migrant people who moved according to the availability of food in different locations during the changing seasons. They passed their knowledge of plants that

were good for eating or healing from one generation to the next.

The skills that made the Apaches successful hunters also made them respected warriors. They excelled at throwing sticks and spears and setting traps to capture wild animals for meat. These skills were important in battle. When trouble developed with other groups of Indians or settlers, their stealth enabled them to approach an enemy camp very quietly to steal horses, food, or weapons without being detected. By the early twentieth century, the Apaches, like other Native American tribes, had been defeated and relegated to reservations in New Mexico and Oklahoma. Some of them avoided capture because of their ability to avoid detection.

When the Cherokee and Apache tribes came to Texas, they moved into areas formerly occupied by the Caddo Indians. Caddo is the name given to a group of tribes who lived in what is now East Texas and surrounding areas. They formed a confederation known as the Tejas, which means, "those who are friends." All of the tribes in the confederation were "friends" with one another and also friendly to the Spanish explorers who came in the seventeen hundreds. It was from the Caddos that Texas received its name and its motto of "Friendship."

The Caddo were descendants of the people who populated Texas in the Early

Ceramic Period (200 B.C. to A.D. 800). They lived in the piney forests of east Texas where they were predominantly farmers. In large clearings in the woods they raised their main foodstuffs of corn, beans, and squash. They also gathered wild plants for food. Pecans, walnuts, acorns, blackberries, persimmons, roots, and many other plants and fruits were plentiful. In addition they hunted deer, turkeys, rabbits, and squirrels in the piney woods.

A special tree, the bois d'arc, grows in the piney forests. It has a very strong and flexible wood, perfect for making bows used in shooting arrows. Since the bois d'arc only grows in certain regions, the Caddos made bows for themselves and for trading with other Indian tribes that did not have this wood. When the Spanish arrived they were impressed with the bowls, chests, and ceremonial objects the Caddo made from the wood growing in their forests.

The Spanish liked the Caddo because they were so civilized and friendly. These Native Americans even used beds and chairs similar to theirs. The DeSoto expedition lived with the Caddo for a period of time around 1541 and, unfortunately, spread many European diseases among them. These diseases ultimately reduced the Caddo population to a great extent. Then there was plenty of room for other Native American tribes who came to Texas when American settlers pushed them westward.

The Comanches were fierce warriors and savvy traders who lived on the Southern Plains that extended from what is now Nebraska to Texas. The biggest problem was that what they had to sell or trade was usually something they had stolen or someone they had kidnapped. The Spanish and other Indian tribes tolerated this kidnapping and stealing for ransom. However, the American settlers who followed the Indians to Texas did not want to pay for the return of their own goods and people.

Once the Comanche obtained horses from the Europeans, they became extremely skilled riders and fighters. They fought the Spanish, keeping them from extending their control farther north. They attacked and stole from settlers and other Indian tribes alike. Then they tried to sell or trade their hostages for things they needed. This angered the settlers, who could not distinguish between the different tribes. Instead, they grouped them all together as Indians. This fueled the growing conflicts between the Native American tribes and the settlers of European ancestry.

Among the tribes that came to the area that is now Texas were the Alabama, the Coushatta, the Shawnee, the Biloxi, and the Creek. These different groups did not have state boundaries as we do now. Rather they traveled to where they could find food and live peaceably. Each time they encountered other peoples, they learned new things and left their own mark. The result is that all of the groups have some similar characteristics and ultimately met similar fates. Many were displaced from their traditional lands and moved to reservations in Oklahoma, Arkansas, or New Mexico where they often lived in less than ideal conditions. The Alabama-Coushatta Indians now have a reservation in Livingston, between Huntsville and Houston in the heart of the big thicket. The 46,000 acres of land that make up the reservation is land given to them by Sam Houston as a reward for staying neutral when Texas was fighting for its independence from Mexico. Today on the reservation the Indians perform traditional ceremonies and dances for visitors. It is also a recreational area where outsiders can camp and enjoy nature as well as learn about these Native Americans.

When the Indians were moved to the reservations, the United States attempted to take a census. Recording the names proved to be extremely difficult because only the Cherokees had an alphabet, and even that one has characters different from the English alphabet. The government representatives not only could not spell the names of the Indians, frequently they could not even understand or pronounce them. So they recorded a name that seemed similar to what they heard or just gave them a name they could spell. That is how Marvin Johnson's family got their last name. Unfortunately, their original name has been lost.

Within the last couple of generations, the Native Americans have experienced a resurgence of pride in their heritage and culture. The number of powwows and other Native American gatherings has increased dramatically in recent years.

Over the years, people from the different tribes have intermarried with one another and with others. Now there are very few people with a heritage of only one Indian nation. The traditions of the different groups have thus been commingled. Dances, songs, and ceremonies belong to all Native Americans today, rather than to the individual tribe that may have originated it. Today, Native Americans can be found in all walks of life, including the military. Wherever they are and whatever tribe(s) they may be descended from, they gather for powwows and other celebrations. Groups like the Cherokee Cultural Society are active in educating the general public about their heritage. At the same time they are preserving it for future generations.

Native Americans practiced a nature-based religion. Some, like the Caddo, were part of a larger religious culture that is found all across the South and Midwest. They are called mound builders because they built huge earth mounds. The mound in the Fort Davis

area is now preserved as a state park. The mound builders had a special priesthood that cared for the mounds and presided over religious ceremonies. There were also shamans who were healers and magic-makers.

All of the mound builders celebrated seasonal rites called busks. The autumn busk was a kind of harvest festival similar to the type that gave birth to the American holiday of Thanksgiving. Native Americans gave thanks to the earth for her bounty whenever groups gathered. Legends passed from one generation to the next explained the mysteries of the universe. These stories are repeated today at powwows and other gatherings of the tribes, continuing this oral legacy.

Another important facet of the Native American belief system is respect: the respect for others and their differences, even if one disagrees; respect for the past and the need to pass it on to the next generation; and the belief that with respect comes honor.

June 25 of each year is a day that is observed by some Native Americans in Texas today. That is the anniversary date of General Custer's defeat. Although even at the time of the battle the Indians realized that this one victory would not guarantee their fate, it was a moment of encouragement and pride for them. The day is marked by small, simple ceremonies that include the playing of drums and the singing of songs that tell the story of the victory.

Native American celebrations include the use of music and dance. These have also been passed from the elders to the younger generation. Each dance, each cadence of the drums, and each mysterious wail of the flute has a special meaning and tells various stories. Tribal dance competitions with sizeable cash prizes are held throughout Texas and the rest of the country to encourage the younger generation to learn and practice these dances.

The Grass Dance, sometimes called the Victory Dance, was once named the Scalp Dance. Today colorful ribbons or yarn adorn the traditional dress of the dancer rather than scalps of the past. A variation of the Grass Dance is the Dance of the Seventh Plum. According to legend, a young boy who had a lame leg created this dance. He felt sorry for himself because he could not join in the dancing with the others. While alone on a hillside, feeling sorry for himself, his father approached him.

"Don't feel sorry for yourself," his father told him. "That is not our way. Our way is to be proud and to make things happen."

The boy thought about these words and realized that he too could dance; only his dance would be different from the others. He gathered long grasses and horsetails and incorporated them into his regalia. Today when the Dance of the Seventh Plum is performed, the dancers have only one leg on the ground at a time. They kick the other leg in the air just as the lame boy did. The result is an invigorating dance in honor of an ancestor who, though different from the rest, was able to give his own gift of dance. Unlike the lame creator of the Dance of the Seven Plums, the dancers today change legs, being careful to stand on only one leg at a time.

Dancers wear traditional moccasins on their feet. Around their ankles they wear angora fur to impart the spirit of the sure-footed mountain goat to their legs. Bells around the ankles help a group of dancers keep time with the music. When there is a large group of dancers, there is often too much noise for each individual to hear the beat of the drums, but the bells can always be heard. Leggings, once made of skins, are now made of cotton because of the Texas heat.

Indians began painting their faces to intimidate the enemy. If both warring tribes were evenly matched, intimidation might be the determining factor that gave one tribe the edge (and with it the victory) over the other. Today, some paint their faces according to how they feel at the time, while others use the traditional patterns that have been gifted to them.

When an older person passes a part of his heritage by teaching it to a younger one, it is considered a gift. Styles of dress or face painting, songs or dances, and stories from the past are gifts that are passed on from one generation to the next. To be chosen to receive a gift of a dance or a style of face painting is considered a great honor to be cherished forever. Once one has been gifted with a dance or other piece of heritage, it is the receiver's responsibility to use it or perform it and then to pass it on by teaching it to others.

And that is just what Greg Howard is doing every Tuesday night—gifting to others his ancestral language.

Native American Recipes

Native Americans ate whatever was available. They knew which plants were edible and which needed to be cooked and which did not. Typically, they prepared a large pot of some sort of stew that would simmer throughout the day. It was always available for whenever anyone got hungry. On special feast days and at ceremonies, a banquet-type meal would be served. Most of these occasions were a form of thanksgiving to mother earth for her abundance.

Small game like rabbits and squirrels were often prepared by skinning and then roasting over a fire or boiling in an oven or pot. Sometimes they were packed in mud and buried under the fire. Once cooked, the skin of the animal could easily be pulled off, taking with it all the mud and dirt.

The Indians ate the nuts, fruits, and vegetables that they found growing in the wild. These foods were eaten in their natural state, just as they are today. The corn, beans, and squash that the Indians learned to cultivate long before the arrival of Europeans were staples in their diet. Even today, these are popular ingredients in their food.

Indian Ceremonial Dish

Delicious anytime, not just for ceremonies!

4   cups beef or pork broth—homemade, canned, or instant

¾-1 cup cornmeal

1   teaspoon sage

½   teaspoon salt

1   small onion, chopped (optional)

Strain the broth if it is homemade. Boil the salt, sage, and onion in the broth until the onion is tender. Slowly pour the cornmeal into simmering broth, stirring constantly. Simmer until very thick. Pour into a jellyroll pan, cool, then slice.

Venison and Wild Rice Stew

Deer and wild rice are both still plentiful. Deer hunting is a popular Texas sport in the fall, but venison is also readily available in many grocery stores. Wild rice is also in most grocery stores. Ironically, even though a lot of rice is cultivated in Texas, the wild rice available in stores today is usually from a northern state.

3½ pounds venison, cut into 2-inch cubes
1½ teaspoons salt
⅛ teaspoon fresh ground pepper
2 yellow onions, peeled and quartered
1½ cups wild rice

Simmer the venison, onions, and water to cover in a large uncovered pot for 3 hours or until the meat is tender. Add the remaining ingredients, cover, and simmer for about 45 minutes. Add additional water here if needed to cover all ingredients. Stir and simmer uncovered for another 20 minutes or until the rice is tender and most of the liquid is absorbed.

Note: Beef or bison can be substituted for the venison.

Quick-cooking wild rice mixes can also be used. Because of the high salt content in these, do not add the salt until near the end. Then salt to taste. Also, decrease the cooking time if processed rice is used.

Indian Chile Casserole

1 can (15 oz.) whole kernel corn
2 cans (15 oz.) hominy
1 or 2 small cans (4 oz.) chopped green chile, according to taste
2 cups sour cream
3½ cups shredded cheddar cheese

Drain and dry the corn and hominy. Mix everything together except for ½ c. cheese. Bake in greased casserole for 30-40 minutes at 350°. Sprinkle the remaining cheese over the top. Bake for 10-15 minutes more until cheese is melted and lightly brown.

Note: You can use white or yellow hominy or one can of each. Shredded Monterey Jack cheese can be substituted for some or all of the cheddar.

Cherokee Bean Balls

1 can (16 oz.) brown beans
½ cup water
2 cups cornmeal
¼ cup flour
½ teaspoon baking soda

Heat the beans to boiling. Add up to ½ cup water if necessary. Mix the dry ingredients in a large bowl. Add the beans and water and mix well, using your hands.

Roll into about 20 balls. Drop in boiling water. Cook for 30 minutes at a slow boil.

Note: These can be served as dumplings in a hearty soup. They can also be served as a side dish to hearty grilled meats. For vegetarian meals, these make a tasty main entree. Serve with mustard or picante sauce.

Fry Bread

A delicious staple in the Indian diet!

2 cups flour
2 teaspoons baking powder
½ teaspoon salt
1 cup milk
Oil for frying

Mix everything except oil. Knead the dough on a floured surface until it is soft and easy to handle. Pat or roll until dough is about ⅓ inch thick. Cut into squares or shape into circles. Fry in hot oil until golden brown. Turn and fry the other side.

Note: These can be used for making tacos instead of tortillas. Or the fry bread can be used for the foundation of any type of sandwich, hot or cold. Fry bread is also a delicious snack or dessert served hot sprinkled with powdered sugar or sugar and cinnamon or with honey.

Finger Bread

This is based on a recipe for corn bread given to early Czech settlers by the Eden Indians.

1   cup yellow cornmeal
¼   teaspoon salt
½   teaspoon baking powder
½   cup boiling water
oil for frying

Pour water over the dry ingredients to barely moisten. Let stand for one minute.

With damp hands, shape into finger-size pieces, not more than ½ inch thick. Fry in oil until brown.

Note: Minced dried onion or bacon bits can be added to the corn bread, if desired.

Fried Hominy

6   slices bacon, cut into pieces
2   cans (16 oz.) hominy, drained
⅛   teaspoon pepper
½   teaspoon salt (optional)
2   green onions, sliced thin (including tops)

Fry the bacon pieces until crisp. Stir in hominy, and heat for 5 minutes. Add salt, pepper, and green onions. Heat for an additional 5 minutes.

Cherokee Berry Bread

1 egg
1 cup sugar
1 stick butter (8 tablespoons)
2 cups self-rising flour
1 cup milk
1 teaspoon vanilla
2 cups berries

Cream together egg, sugar, and butter. Add flour, milk, and vanilla. Sprinkle a little flour on the berries to prevent them from sinking to the bottom of the batter. Fold in the berries. Pour into a 9-inch square or round pan that has been sprayed with a nonstick cooking spray. Bake at 350° for 40 minutes or until done.

Note: Blueberries, blackberries, huckleberries, or other berries may used.

Yellow Jacket Soup

Yellow jacket soup was considered a delicious delicacy. Only the bravest dared gather the main ingredient!

1 nest of ground-dwelling yellow jackets (must be full of grubs)
Water
Seasonings to taste
Oil, butter, or margarine for frying

Loosen the uncovered grubs by heating them and removing them from the nest. Heat the nest with the remaining grubs over a fire until the thin paper-like covering parches. Pick out the yellow jackets. Be extremely careful! Brown the yellow jackets in the oil or butter. Cook the browned yellow jackets in boiling water to make soup. Season to taste.

Note: I have not personally tried making this soup. If any reader should try this recipe, please let me know the results.

Lasting Influence—
Mexicans in Texas

On Saturday nights, the River Walk in San Antonio is bustling with mariachis serenading tourists sitting at sidewalk cafes drinking margaritas and munching on nachos. A floating Mexican restaurant slips by on the calm waters of the canal off the San Antonio River. The diners enjoy the constantly changing scenery as they indulge in a variety of delicious Tex-Mex specialties. Just up the steps to street level is the Alamo and the rest of Texas where so much of the Mexican culture is now integrated into what we sometimes just call "Texan." All the other groups who came afterwards have adopted much of what the Mexicans brought to Texas.

Even the most popular image of Texas—the cowboy—is from the *vaquero* of the Spanish and Mexican periods. The saddle, chaps, lasso, spurs, and such were from the *vaqueros*. After the Civil War when the large herds of longhorns were rounded up and branded then driven to market, these items from the *vaqueros* were generally adopted by the Anglos. This image of the Texas cowboy supercedes almost all other ideas of our state.

The Spanish were the first outsiders to come to what is now the Southwest United States, Mexico, and Central America. What we consider to be Mexican traditions are largely a combination of Spanish and Indian. The Spaniards brought Christianity to the New World in the form of Catholicism. Many of the Aztec traditions were blended into the new Christian beliefs to form new traditions that are still practiced today in both Texas and Mexico.

One of these is *El Día de los Muertos*—the Day of the Dead. November 1 is All Souls' Day in the Catholic Church. This is a time for prayer and for respectful remembrance of the departed. The Day of the Dead, which is celebrated on November 1 also, evolved from the All Soul's remembrances combined with Aztec rituals that sought to link the living with their departed ancestors. Marigolds and scented candles are used to ritually summon the spirits for a feast. Small altars at home are decorated with papier-mâché skeletons and candy skulls. The candy skulls may be made at home or, more likely, bought at a specialty store and painted by family members. An offering, often something the deceased particularly liked, such as cigarettes or a stuffed toy, is placed on the altar also. This is a time of great joy for Mexican families, not a time for sorrow. Families go to the cemetery to party with the dead and to laugh at death. This allows the dead to live again, if just for a short time, in the hearts of those who still remember. This helps take the fear out of death. The early Spanish priests infused Catholic theology into this Aztec ceremony. Today, it is part of the Mexican culture that is still celebrated in Texas—not just by those of Mexican heritage, but also by many of Indian heritage.

Another custom that is now Mexican but originated with the Spaniards and Indians is the *quinceañera*. This is the custom of celebrating a girl's fifteenth birthday and her entrance into adulthood. It is an elaborate affair that combines coming of age rituals with the sacraments of the Church. Originally, the *quinceañera* marked when a young girl was ready for marriage. Of course, today society does not consider a fifteen-year-old girl old enough to get married. Instead of being a coming-out party, the *quinceañera* is an elaborate birthday party based on an old custom. It marks a special time in a girl's life when she is considered old enough to take on more responsibilities in her own life and in the affairs of the family and the community.

At her *quinceañera* the girl marches down the middle of the aisle of the church. Her attendants, who are also about fifteen years old, follow her. The ceremony includes a special mass when the honoree renews her commitment to Christian values. The young woman wears a beautiful white dress similar to a wedding dress, a religious medal to represent her faith, a ring for spiritual and communal responsibilities, and a crown that foreshadows her triumph in living a Christian life. She carries flowers to represent new life. The flowers are presented to the Virgin Mary in thanks for keeping her from bodily harm. At the end of the mass, young men escort the girls from the church.

A party follows the religious portion of the celebration. Because this is very expensive, relatives and friends often help by becoming a sponsor or *madrina*. To be asked to be a *madrina* is considered to be an honor and a blessing. The *madrinas* take their role very seriously and try to do their best for the honoree. Social responsibility dictates that the more one has, the more one must give back. Being a *madrina* enables one to do just that. The dress *madrina* is often someone who sews and can provide the dress; the food *madrina* may be someone who caters and can

provide the food, etc. Like all birthday parties, the guests all bring gifts to the girl.

In recent years, some areas have encouraged several girls to share their *quinceañera* in order to spread the costs of the party over more families. The Church is trying to stress the religious portion of the ceremony, rather than the secular, to return the *quinceañera* to its original form. However, like all traditions, some are bypassing the *quinceañera* as an outdated social custom. Still others are reviving it after a period of time when many traditions were neglected.

The next major event in a girl's life is her wedding. Three things are essential at a Hispanic wedding. The first of these is the *arras*. This is thirteen dimes the groom gives to his bride. It represents his pledge to work and provide for her. Before giving the dimes to his bride, the man gives them to the priest to bless. The next essential element is the lasso, which is a special gift often given to the bride by her attendants. The lasso is a large rosary with two circles joined together with a cross in the middle. One circle is placed over the head of each so it rests on the couple's shoulders. The cross on the rosary hangs between them. It represents the couple coming together as one. The bridal couple wears the lasso throughout the wedding mass. The last element is the unity candle that represents the couple leaving their original family and forming their own new one. In the old days, the bride took her flowers to the

Virgin Mary to thank her for keeping her a virgin until her wedding day.

After the ceremony the wedding dinner is served. Usually the menu includes a special chicken dish, rice, beans, chile, and pico de gallo. Of course other favorite foods will be on the menu, also. But regardless of what is served, the banquet will feature more than enough delicious food for everyone.

Often the bride will carry a handkerchief that will later be made into a baptismal hat for her baby to wear. Babies are generally baptized when they are quite young, rarely more than six months old, and usually much sooner. The child will have godparents to promise to raise the child in the Church if something should happen to the parents. After the religious ceremony, a celebration including all the friends and relatives follows.

The main events in a child's life revolve around the Church—baptism, first communion, confirmation, *quienceañera*, and marriage. Each of these ceremonies is a group effort made possible by *madrinas* who accept the honor and help plan and pay for the celebration. Like with the *quinceañera*, different parts of the wedding may have *madrinas*. Once again, it is considered a huge honor to be asked to be a part of the festivities.

Christmas is a special time of feasting and worshipping. Each family always has its own favorites, but the meal will inevitably include tamales and buñuelos. Tamales are served again on New Year's Eve. They are extremely time-consuming to make, and therefore they are only made at home for special occasions. (There is no recipe for tamales in this book because I could not figure out how to streamline them so they would be practical to make at home. Place your order early and let someone else do all the work!) Buñuelos are a type of Mexican doughnut that is delicious and much easier to make. They are especially good served with Mexican hot chocolate after midnight mass, an important tradition for most families.

During the night Santa Claus (or perhaps Papá Noel) comes to leave toys and surprises for the children, just as he does in households throughout Texas and the United States. In addition to this secular interval, Hispanics try to remember the religious side of Christmas. On Christmas morning the family will pray the rosary together and lay the baby Jesus in the *nacimiento*, or manger scene, to represent His birth. The baby stays there until Epiphany when the three kings come. Then the family will pray the rosary again and remove the baby from the manger. Some lucky children receive gifts from the kings on this day also.

La Fiesta de las Luminarias (the Festival of Lights) began as a religious ceremony, lighting the way for Mary and Joseph. Originally, small bonfires lighted the way. In almost every neighborhood at Christmastime, at least one house will have luminaries lighting the walkway to the house. Traditionally, the luminaries were made by filling a brown paper bag about half full with sand and placing a candle inside. Now they are more likely to be lighted with electric lights and to be made of something less flammable, like ceramic.

The next major religious holiday of the year after Christmas is Easter. One of the interesting parts of the Mexican celebration is the *cascarones*, or confetti eggs. These are eggshells that are filled with colorful confetti. Bright crêpe paper or tissue paper covers the large hole in the eggshell where the confetti is put in. Children love to play with these, cracking them open on their friends' heads or tossing them like snowballs to splatter confetti over the target. Sometimes the *cascarones* are painted and decorated like other Easter eggs. Since these are so much fun and so easy to make, school carnivals all over the state sell these as a fundraiser!

At any celebration there is likely to be a piñata. Piñatas are animal, star, or some other shape made out of papier-mâché and decorated with colored paper. Inside the hollow center are small toys and candies. The piñata is hung by a rope from a tree, and one blindfolded player after another tries to break it by swinging a bat. Of course, someone pulls on the rope to raise the piñata out of reach. When someone does

finally break the piñata, everyone scrambles for the prizes that spill to the ground.

Two uniquely Mexican celebrations are called the *Fiestas Patrias*. Both of these originated in the nineteenth century to commemorate historical events. The first one, *Cinco de Mayo* (May 5), commemorated the victory in 1862 in Puebla, Mexico. The second and most important of the two is *Diez y Seis de Septiembre* (September 16), commemorating the call for the defeat of Spanish rule in Mexico in 1810.

Diez y Seis is the national Independence Day in Mexico. It is celebrated throughout Texas with three-day events that include parades with elaborate floats depicting important events in Mexican history. A queen is selected to represent the Virgin of Guadalupe, the ancient goddess and modern patron saint of Mexico. In addition, a princess and duchess are also selected. Much of the revelry, dancing, singing, and partying revolve around the selection of the royal court. Fireworks on September 17 officially conclude the celebration.

Cinco de Mayo is the festival next in importance. This celebrates the recall of the French Maximilian and Carlota and the defeat of the French forces in Mexico in 1862. In addition, *Cinco de Mayo* also celebrates the cultural ties shared by Mexican Americans with each other and with Mexico. Parades, dances, and other forms of celebration mark this day in a number of different cities throughout Texas. The *Fiestas Patrias*, like the Juneteenth celebration by African Americans, are celebrations designed to preserve the multiethnic roots in Texas.

It was only a little over a decade after Mexico won its independence from Spain that Texas won its independence from Mexico. You would think that all Mexicans would fight on their country's side when we struggled for independence. However, there were at least seven Mexicans who died defending the Alamo. Just as the Mexicans had become frustrated under Spanish rule, the Texians (combination of Texas and Mexican) felt a growing dissatisfaction with the central government so far away in Mexico City. The ultimate annexation to the United States was not the end they envisioned, however.

The Mexican influence is felt throughout Texas in our language, architecture, and community celebrations. Throughout the state cities and towns have fiestas and piñatas. Almost every town has at least one Mexican restaurant that actually serves Tex-Mex, a combining of Texas and Mexican foods. Tortillas and jalapeños are universally available throughout the state. Many Mexican traditions are now mainstream Texan!

Mexican Recipes

I have purposely kept the heat level in these recipes mild. If you want to turn up the spiciness, add additional chiles, chili sauce, or dried chili powder to suit your own tastes.

Picante Sauce

2   cans (4 oz.) chopped black olives

1-2 cans (4 oz.) chopped green chiles

1   can (28 oz.) diced tomatoes

1   bunch green onions, diced

2   teaspoons garlic salt

1   teaspoon salt (or less)

1   teaspoon pepper

4   tablespoons olive oil

3   tablespoons wine vinegar

Mix all the ingredients together and refrigerate several hours before serving.

Note: Four firm, fresh tomatoes, peeled and diced, can be used instead of the canned tomatoes. For variety, add one or more of the following: 1 Tbsp. minced fresh cilantro, 1 cup small salad shrimp, or ½ c. diced yellow tomato or bell pepper.

Empanaditas
(Meat-filled Pastries)

1½ cups leftover cooked meat
½   teaspoon habanera pepper sauce
1-2 tablespoons chopped green chiles
¼   cup sour cream
1   9-inch frozen deep dish pie pastry

Chop or shred the meat into small pieces. Add the pepper sauce and chiles to taste. Add enough sour cream to form a thick filling that will hold together. Roll out the pastry and cut into rounds about 2-3 inches in diameter. Place a spoonful of the filling in the center of each pastry. Fold over and seal the edges with a fork. Place the *empanaditas* on a cookie sheet that has been sprayed with a nonstick spray. Bake at 400° for about 15 minutes or until golden.

Note: A half-pound of cooked and drained Mexican sausage is also very good in this recipe.

Corn Relish

This is an easy recipe to double or triple if you need a large quantity for a party.

1½ cups frozen corn kernels
¼   cup well-drained sweet pickle relish
½   cup chopped black olives
½   cup sliced celery
½   teaspoon salt
2   tablespoons sugar
2   tablespoons wine vinegar
5   tablespoons salad oil

Combine the corn, pickle relish, olives, and celery. Dissolve the salt and sugar in the vinegar. Add the salad oil. Cover and shake or mix thoroughly. Pour over the corn mixture. Chill for several hours, stirring occasionally.

Note: This can be served with tortilla chips as a dip, mixed with lettuce as a salad, or as a side dish.

Tortilla Chips

8   corn or flour tortillas

Cut the tortillas into eight wedges. Spray a large cookie sheet with cooking spray. Lay the tortilla wedges in a single layer on the pan. Spray with the cooking spray. Bake at 400° until golden, about 5 minutes. Turn the chips over and bake until the second side is golden.

Corn Bread

1   cup cornmeal
1½ teaspoons baking powder
½   teaspoon salt
2   eggs
⅔   cup melted butter or margarine
1   cup sour cream
2   cups corn kernels (frozen or canned)
¼   pound grated cheese (Monterey Jack, cheddar, or a combination of the two)
1   can (4 oz.) chopped green chiles

Mix dry ingredients together. Make a well in the center. Add the eggs, butter, and sour cream in the well. Blend thoroughly. Stir in the corn. Pour the batter into a greased or sprayed 9-inch pan or skillet. Top with the cheese and chiles. Bake at 375° for 30-40 minutes.

Note: Adjust the chiles to taste.

Tortillas

I never thought I would go to all the work to make my own tortillas. But after trying this recipe, I now know why homemade tortillas are worth the effort!

2   cups instant corn masa mix
1¼ cups water

Mix the masa and water together until it forms a firm ball of dough. Use a tortilla press if you have one or flatten a small ball of dough with your hands. Put it between two sheets of plastic wrap or waxed paper. Use a rolling pin to further flatten and smooth the tortilla. If desired use a small pan lid as a "cookie" cutter so all the tortillas will be the same size. Cook each tortilla in a hot, ungreased skillet for about 20-30 seconds on each side. The tortillas are now ready to be eaten or used in another recipe.

Note: If you are going to eat the tortilla as is, lightly fry them in butter, margarine, or oil.

Arroz Con Tomate
(Mexican Rice)

A classic dish!

2   tablespoons olive oil
½   cup diced green bell pepper
¼   cup finely chopped onion
1   clove garlic, minced
½   teaspoon basil
½   teaspoon rosemary
1   cup rice
1   cup peeled and chopped tomato
    (drained if canned or fresh)
½   teaspoon salt
⅛   teaspoon pepper
2   cups water

Sauté the bell pepper, onion, garlic, basil, and rosemary in oil until tender. Stir in rice, tomato, salt, pepper, and water. Cover and cook over low heat for about 20 minutes until rice is done.

Salbutes

Tortilla dough (see recipe above, but do not cook)

Butter, margarine, or oil for frying

Toppings:

frijoles

shredded lettuce

diced tomatoes

diced cucumbers

thinly sliced red onions

shredded chicken

shredded cheese

diced black olives

sliced green olives

Roll the tortilla dough until it is about ⅛ inch thick. Cut into rounds about 3 inches in diameter. (The top of a large glass or jar works great for this.) Fry in oil until golden on each side. Drain on paper towels. Top with frijoles, lettuce, tomatoes, cucumbers, and cheese for vegetarian salbutes. Top with lettuce, chicken, red onion, tomato, and avocado for chicken salbutes. Make up your own combinations of toppings. Garnish with salsa, sour cream, and lemon juice.

Note: These are great as an appetizer or for a light supper.

Kids like them because you can pick them up and eat them with your hands!

Enchiladas Con Pollo
(Chicken Enchiladas)

This is a great make-ahead recipe. Assemble the enchiladas and refrigerate until shortly before time to eat. A great treat for guests!

1	tablespoon flour
1	cup chicken broth
2	cups cream or milk
2	green onions with tops, chopped
¾	teaspoon salt
¾	teaspoon pepper
2	cups sour cream
12	flour tortillas
3	cups cooked, shredded chicken
1	cup diced pimientos
½	pound sharp cheddar cheese, grated

Mix the flour with the chicken broth in a skillet and heat until slightly thickened. Add the cream, onions, salt, and pepper. Bring to a boil. Remove from heat and stir in the sour cream until well mixed. Dip a tortilla into this mixture, then arrange chicken and a half teaspoon pimiento down the center. Roll up the enchilada and place in a greased baking dish. Repeat with all 12 tortillas. Pour the remaining sour cream mixture over the enchiladas. Bake at 350° for 30 minutes. Sprinkle with cheese and heat until the cheese melts.

Serve with hot salsa for those who want extra fire!

Note: Buttermilk can be substituted for some or all of the sour cream.

Flautas
(Fried Filled Tortillas)

12 tortillas

1½ cups cooked chicken or beef

½   teaspoon habanera pepper sauce
    (optional)

Oil for frying

Garnishes:

shredded lettuce

diced tomatoes

salsa

sour cream

guacamole

Sprinkle a little water on one tortilla. Wrap the tortilla in a paper towel and heat it in the microwave for 15-20 seconds. Shred the meat. Mix in the pepper sauce, if desired. Place a narrow pile of filling along the center of tortilla. Roll and secure with a toothpick. Repeat until all 12 tortillas have been filled and rolled.

Heat the oil in a large, heavy skillet. Fry the *flautas*, turning to brown evenly. Drain on paper towels. Remove the toothpicks. Serve with lettuce, tomatoes, salsa, sour cream, or guacamole for dipping, as desired.

Tequila/Beer Chili

If you like mild chili, halve the spices and then add to taste.

2½ pounds chili meat
2   green bell peppers, diced
1   onion, diced
2   tablespoons tequila
1   cup beer
1   cup diced canned tomatoes
¼   cup cumin
¼   cup chili powder
2   tablespoons paprika
1   tablespoon cayenne pepper
1   tablespoon salt
2   tablespoons powdered mustard

Sauté the meat and onions until the meat is brown and the onion is transparent. Add the bell peppers and sauté for a few minutes more. Add the remaining ingredients. Simmer until the meat is tender and the smell is irresistible! Serve with grated cheese, chopped green onions, sliced avocado, tortilla chips, warm tortillas, or rice.

Note: Chili-ground beef or venison or a combination of the two is great in this recipe.

Grandma Techa's Menudo

My friend Rosalie Rodriguez of San Antonio gave this recipe to me. It is one of her favorites and has been in her family for generations.

5   pounds tripe

1-1½ pounds beef soup bone

1   teaspoon salt

½   head of fresh garlic

1   large can (32 oz.) white hominy, drained

1   small can (16 oz.) white hominy, drained

1   bag of menudo mix (Bolner's-Fiesta is a good brand to use)

1   package dry ancho red chile peppers, seeded and chopped in a blender

Wash each piece of tripe with a brush before cooking. Cut into bite-size pieces and boil 20 minutes. Discard the water and repeat three times more. The last time you boil the tripe, add the remaining ingredients and boil for 3½ hours. Serve with chopped onion, sliced lemon, and warm corn tortillas.

Note: Open the window during the first three boilings!

According to myth, this is very good for a hangover, especially if eaten in the wee hours of the morning.

Quelites
(Steamed Spinach)

1   package frozen chopped spinach (16 oz.)

3   tablespoons chopped onion

1   slice bacon

Dash ground red chile

½   teaspoon salt

Cook the spinach according to package directions. Cut the bacon into small pieces. Fry the bacon and sauté the onion in a large skillet. Add the spinach, ground red chile, and salt. Mix together. Heat for an additional 5 minutes.

Note: Fresh spinach or any kind of greens can be used.

If you use dried minced onion instead of fresh, add it to the spinach rather than to the bacon.

Elote
(Corn Custard)

This is almost like a corn soufflé. It is creamy, smooth, and delicious.

1 cup frozen corn
1 cup milk
1 teaspoon baking powder
1 teaspoon salt
Dash of pepper
1 tablespoon sugar
3 eggs

Put all the ingredients in a blender or food processor bowl. Whirl until everything is well blended. Pour into a greased or sprayed 1-quart baking dish. Bake at 350° for 40-60 minutes or until a knife inserted in the center comes out clean.

Note: Fresh or canned corn can also be used.

Mexican Wedding Cakes

The name may say "cake," but these are really cookies that are great with coffee or tea. They are similar to sand tarts.

2 cups flour
¼ cup sugar
¼ teaspoon salt
1 cup butter or margarine
2 teaspoons vanilla
2 cups finely chopped pecans
½ cup powdered sugar

Mix together the flour, sugar, and salt. In a large bowl, mix the butter into the dry ingredients. Add the vanilla and nuts. Shape dough into ½-inch balls. Place 1 inch apart on a lightly greased or sprayed cookie sheet. Bake at 325° for about 20 minutes or until lightly browned. While still warm, roll in powdered sugar.

Queso Napolitano

Virginia Concho, a wonderful cook, prepared this for me and I had to have the recipe! This recipe is for the best flan I have ever eaten. It is incredibly rich and wonderful!

1   cup milk
10 eggs
1   can (14 oz.) sweetened condensed milk
½   cup sugar
1   teaspoon vanilla

Heat the sugar until it turns into a clear brown liquid. Pour it into a 9-inch round metal cake pan and swirl it around until the entire bottom is covered. Work quickly. Cool. Beat the milk, condensed milk, and eggs until well mixed. Pour over the caramelized sugar in the cake pan. Fill a large skillet about halfway with water. Place the cake pan with the custard in the water. Cover and cook for about an hour at a medium-low heat.

When a knife inserted in the center comes out clean, the custard is ready. Cool. Place a serving plate over the top of the custard and turn upside down. The custard should slide out of the pan. Sprinkle the vanilla on top. Refrigerate and serve when cold.

Buñuelos

¾ cup milk

4 tablespoons butter or margarine

1 tablespoon aniseed, crushed

½ teaspoon salt

2 beaten eggs

3 cups flour

1 teaspoon baking powder

Oil for frying

Topping:

Scald the milk. Add the butter, aniseed, and salt. Remove from heat and allow to cool to room temperature. Stir in the eggs. Mix the flour and egg mixtures together. Knead the dough until smooth. Shape the dough into about 20 balls. Cover and let rest for 10 minutes. Roll each ball into a 4-inch circle. Fry, one at a time, in the oil until golden on each side. Be sure to keep the waiting dough covered.

Use one of the following toppings:

Cinnamon and sugar topping:

½ cup sugar

1 teaspoon cinnamon

Mix the cinnamon and sugar together in a plastic bag. Gently shake each warm buñuelo in the sugar mixture.

Warm Syrup:

6 tablespoons brown sugar

½ cup hot water

½ cup light sherry

½ cup seedless raisins

1 teaspoon cinnamon

⅛ teaspoon maple flavoring (optional)

Combine all the ingredients in a saucepan and boil until slightly thickened. Soak in the syrup or serve the syrup for dunking.

Pralines

2½ cups sugar

1 cup buttermilk

1 teaspoon baking soda

⅛ teaspoon salt

¼ cup butter or margarine

1 teaspoon vanilla

3 cups pecan halves

Heat the sugar, buttermilk, soda, and salt until the sugar dissolves, stirring frequently. Continue cooking over low heat to soft ball stage or 234°. Remove from heat and add butter and vanilla. Cool about 5 minutes. Beat until smooth and slightly thick. Stir in pecans. Drop immediately from a tablespoon onto waxed paper.

Note: Do not make on a humid day.

Tortilla Soup

An all-time favorite recipe! Delicious on a cold night or anytime!

1 medium onion, chopped

1 tablespoon chopped green chiles (canned)

3 cloves garlic, chopped

6 strips bacon

1 can (10¾ oz.) condensed beef bouillon

3 cans (10¾ oz.) condensed chicken broth

6 cups water

2 teaspoons cumin

2 teaspoons chili powder

4 teaspoons Worcestershire sauce

2 tablespoons soy sauce

1 cup shredded chicken

1 cup shredded cheddar cheese

1 avocado, thinly sliced

Sauté the bacon, chiles, onion, and garlic together until the onions are transparent and the bacon is crisp. Set the bacon aside. Add the bouillon, water, cumin, chili powder, Worcestershire sauce, and soy sauce. Bring the soup to boiling. Add the chicken and crumbled bacon, lower the heat, and simmer covered for about an hour. Serve the soup in bowls with crisp tortilla strips, sliced avocado (optional), and grated cheese.

Note: Make tortilla chips (recipe on page 20), except cut the tortillas into strips rather than wedges.

Mexican Coffee

1 teaspoon cinnamon
½ cup dark brown sugar
8 level tablespoons coffee grounds
Water for 8 cups of coffee

Add the cinnamon and sugar to the coffee grounds. Brew the coffee as you usually do.

Note: Strong, dark roast coffee is best to use in this recipe.

For a festive touch, top with a spoonful of whipping cream.

For added punch, add kahlúa to taste and top with whipping cream.

Miniature Piñata Ornament for the Christmas Tree

2 paper cups with rolled rims and pointed bottoms
gold or silver spray paint
paint pens of different colors or other paint
pipe cleaner
tapestry needle
heavy-duty thread

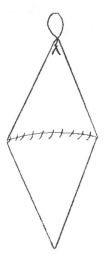

Insert the end of the pipe cleaner through the pointed end of one cup. Curve the end to make a hook. Spread the end of the pipe cleaner inside the cup so it won't pull through. Place the rims of the two cups together. Stitch the cups together with the needle and thread. Spray with the spray paint. When dry, decorate with colorful designs. Use your imagination!

Cascarones
(Confetti Eggs)

clean, empty egg shells
confetti
colored tissue paper
glue or paste

Carefully crack the eggs at one end so at least ¾ of the eggshell remains intact. Wash the eggshell completely. Be sure to remove all the inner membrane. Let dry. Fill the eggshell with confetti. Glue a strip of the colored tissue paper over the hole so the confetti will not fall out. Decorate the eggshells with colored pens, if desired.

Note: Children and adults love cracking these over friends' heads. Just be sure to do it outside!

From Across the Continent or Across the Sea—

Celtic Customs in Texas

You do not have to be Irish to drink green beer on St. Patrick's Day—or even know that this is the day to honor the patron saint of Ireland. Nor do you have to be British to eat roast beef or Scottish to wear plaid. Many of the early English-speaking immigrants to Texas, especially during Mexican rule, came from the United States. Some of these early settlers were second- or third-generation Americans. Rather than being English or Scottish or Irish, they arrived in Texas as Americans. Even today, regardless of whatever mixed blood we may have in our veins, all Americans (Texans included!) enjoy a colorful group heritage from the English and their Celtic cousins.

The groups of immigrants from the British Isles, namely the Scots, the Welsh, and the Irish, came to Texas with the same dreams as other immigrants in the nineteenth century. Unlike other groups, however, they already spoke the language and therefore had more opportunities available to them than those who did not. This enabled them to help already established cities and towns to grow and develop into what they are today. Many of the shared traditions of all these related groups have evolved to become imbedded in the American culture. Of all the Anglos who came to Texas after the Civil War, the Irish came in the greatest numbers.

Texas and Ireland have had a long history together. The Irish have always left their homeland to seek their fortune elsewhere. Texas is one place that has always attracted adventurous people. So the Irish came here as early as the seventeen hundreds when Texas was still under Spanish rule. In 1777 an Irish priest, Juan Augustin Morfi, wrote one of the earliest and best accounts of Texas—the land and the people—in his *History of Texas.*

Prior to the Texas Revolution against Mexico, small groups of Irish families settled in Texas. Two Irishmen, James McGloin and John McMullen, received from Mexico an *empresario* grant to bring colonists to settle along the Nueces River. The two Irishmen traveled to New York to recruit their newly arrived countrymen to come to Texas. Their glowing reports of rich farmland, though based on fact, did not prepare the settlers for what they actually experienced. First, the captain of the ship that brought them to Texas miscalculated the course and missed the planned arrival port. Their arrival at Matagorda Bay was a harbinger of the misfortunes to follow. On their way to their inland destination, they stopped for provisions and to rest at the Mission Refugio. Some Indians paid them a visit and demanded gifts. McMullen adamantly refused, thus ensuring problems. Frightened women and children who had never seen "savages" before refused to leave the stone church. Some wanted to leave and did. But the pull of land ownership enticed others to stay.

Those who stayed waited over three years before various disputes and legal conflicts were resolved and they could proceed. When they finally reached their grant, they found an untamed land covered with tall grass. The only water came from the river, and Indians surrounded them. By this time the frustration level was, not surprisingly, very high, and at this point they were probably asking themselves why they had come. The answer was obvious— land and freedom.

Since these Irish were Catholic and that was the official religion here at the time, the Mexican government viewed them as loyal colonists. Unfortunately for the Mexicans, once the Revolution began, the Irish colonists in what is now the Corpus Christi area became experts in guerrilla warfare. Their attacks on the Mexican army and its supply lines definitely helped the Texans' cause. Even though the Irish had long rebelled against English domination in Ireland, their sympathies in Texas were more with the Anglos (of English descent) from the United States than with the Mexicans. They viewed the Mexicans much as they had the English when they lived in Ireland—as outsiders interfering in self-government.

Irishmen died at the Alamo, fought at San Jacinto, and signed the Goliad Declaration of Independence. However, the true Irish influence in Texas did not begin until after the Civil War when Ireland, like much of Europe, was plagued by famine and economic oppression. Like other immigrants who came to Texas at this time, the Irish were poor and needed jobs. Fortunately, the railroads needed labor that the

newcomers willingly provided. The development of the town of Smithville, the railroad, and the Irish are intertwined in Texas history. They were the ones who originally laid out the plans for the town, farmed the fertile land in the area, and ultimately brought the railroad to the town.

In actuality, the Irish entered most lines of work. It was an artist of Irish descent, Harry Arthur McArdle, who helped create the Texas myths in his paintings of the battles of the Alamo and San Jacinto. Perhaps it was a touch of Irish "blarney" that caused neither painting to be historically accurate, to the advantage of the Texans, of course. Both of these huge paintings hang in the State Capitol at Austin.

When the Irish and the others from the British Isles came to Texas, they brought with them traditions and foods that were heavily influenced by the English who dominated them. In spite of the conflicts in the old country, one of the appeals of Texas was the Anglo influence that permeated Texas. The great influx of settlers from other parts of the United States, many of English, Irish, or Scottish descent, made Texas an English-speaking land with a similar social organization.

The Irish quickly incorporated the new foods they found growing abundantly here. Among these were watermelons, cantaloupes, okra, sweet potatoes, and peppers. And they were delighted to also find abundant beef and game meat here, foods often in short supply in Ireland.

When Irish settlers first came to Texas, they did not celebrate Christmas like the annual Galveston reenactment of "A Dickens of a Christmas." While that may have been a glorified yet somewhat authentic Christmas in England and other parts of the British Empire during that time, it is not how the immigrants celebrated here. Many of their traditions were already practiced here, having been brought by settlers from other parts of the United States.

The burning of the yule log, a tradition imported to the English-speaking world from the Scandinavian countries, continued in Texas. As in the old country, the yule log was always lighted with a bit from the previous year's log. The log had to be a trunk section of a large tree because it was to burn continuously from Christmas to New Year's.

Christmas trees came to Britain from Germany shortly before our Civil War. However, the British decorated their trees more elaborately than did the Germans. When the Irish immigrants celebrated Christmas in their new homes, they wanted evergreen trees also.

New Texans of different backgrounds brought the custom of placing lighted candles in the windows. This dates back to medieval times when the candles represented lighting the way for Mary and Joseph so they could find a place to stay. For the Irish Catholics during the time of English Protestant rule, this tradition provided an alibi for illegal religious worship. Priests would hide in the forests at night to escape persecution. The candles guided them to homes where they were welcome to come in and celebrate mass. Even after the need for the cover story no longer existed, the Irish continued placing candles in the windows.

The Irish were delighted to find mistletoe growing copiously in Texas trees. The Celtic Druids considered mistletoe sacred. Because it was thought to ward off evil spirits, it was hung over all the doors into a house. Young ladies entering a home always had to pass under the mistletoe. Since no evil spirits could enter, kissing under the mistletoe must then be acceptable! The custom of making "kissing balls" of mistletoe and other greens rapidly caught on in Texas. This was the nineteenth century, after all, and a gentleman needed an acceptable excuse to steal a kiss from a girl!

The sending of Christmas cards began in England in the mid-nineteenth century. It quickly caught on in Texas. Cards with a Texas motif—cactus, roadrunners, etc.—became and have continued to be extremely popular.

The Scots brought some special traditions focused on New Year's. Of course, their greatest contribution is Robert Burn's poem "Auld Lang Syne." Though this song did not come directly to Texas from Scotland, it is still sung here and throughout the world. According to Scottish tradition, the first person to set foot across the threshold after midnight on New Year's Day determines the fortune of the house. Some groups of Scots arrange for a tall, dark-haired member to be the first visitor in their homes to assure good luck for the year! If the first person across the threshold is a red-haired woman, terrible things are thought to be in store for the household in the coming year.

Wassail, eggnog, whiskey punch, puddings, and pies were all brought to us from the British Isles. Many of our common recipes came from these people. Whether they came directly from these countries or by way of earlier arrivals, it is hard to say.

The Irish gave us witty blessings and toasts that are still used today. A typical blessing is the marriage blessing:

May God be with you and bless you,
May you see your children's children,
May you be poor in misfortunes,
Rich in blessings,
May you know nothing but happiness
From this day forward.

Today, many events celebrate our group heritage. Renaissance festivals, highland games, and gatherings of the clans are held throughout the state. At these events men wear their tartans and compete in traditional contests. Young

girls may dance around crossed swords. Everyone has a great time listening to bagpipes, exploring genealogy, and experiencing their roots. But these games are a recent attempt to re-create a prior life in Scotland, rather than portraying the life of the Scots in Texas. Just as the Renaissance festivals allow us to experience a colorful part of our group heritage, they do not represent the English when they first came to the new world any more than the games represent the Scottish adventures in Texas.

One attempt to strengthen the bonds between Ireland and Texas is through the Rose of Tyree. Each year a young woman who best represents Irish ideals is chosen in the town of Tyree, Ireland. A young lady from each county in Ireland vies for the title. Candidates from Dallas, Houston, and a few other cities throughout the world compete on an equal footing with the girls from the individual counties in Ireland. The contest is not based on beauty, but rather on personality and Irish ideals such as compassion and communication skills. The bringing together of people from all over the world helps Irish descendants maintain connections with their roots.

Today the descendants of both the Irish and Scots often join together in Texas for special celebrations. Celtic music and dancing is popular with both groups. Intermarriage both before and after these groups came to Texas often makes them indistinguishable. After all, this is the Lone Star State where it is possible to remember our roots, but knowing that whatever else we might be, we are Texans!

Irish Recipes

Like the warmth of the sun
And the light of the day,
May the luck of the Irish
Shine bright on your way.

—Irish blessing

Irish Potato Soup

2 tablespoons butter or margarine

1 sliced onion

1 pound peeled potatoes, sliced

1½ cups milk

2-3 cups chicken broth

¼ teaspoon celery seed

¼ teaspoon dried thyme

½ cup light cream or milk

Salt and pepper to taste

1 tablespoon flour

3 tablespoons chopped green onions, including the green tops (optional) or chives

3 tablespoons crumbled crisp bacon (optional)

3 tablespoons shredded cheese (optional)

Cook the onion in half of the butter until transparent. Do not brown. Add potatoes, milk, broth, celery seed, and thyme. Cover and simmer 1 hour. Melt the remaining butter with the flour. Put into the soup to help thicken. Cook for 10 minutes. Blend in a food processor until smooth. Add the cream and reheat. Do not boil. Garnish with the green onion or chives, crumbled bacon, and cheese, if desired.

Note: To make the soup richer, use heavy cream or sour cream instead of light cream.

Boxty
(Potato Pancakes)

This recipe is from Diane McCartney, who kindly shared some of her favorite recipes with me.

3 potatoes

1 tablespoon flour

1 tablespoon cream or milk

1 egg, slightly beaten

1 teaspoon salt

1 small onion, grated

Bacon grease, butter, or margarine for frying

Grate the potatoes in a food processor. Dry thoroughly. Add the flour, cream, egg, salt, and onion and mix well. Fry in butter or bacon fat until golden on each side.

Beef in Guinness

2½ pounds stew meat, cubed
2 tablespoons flour
2 tablespoons butter or margarine
2 large onions, chopped
6 medium carrots, cut
1 cup Guinness beer
1 cup water
Parsley for garnish

Toss the beef with the flour. Brown the beef in the butter. Remove the beef from the pan and brown the onions. Return the beef to the pan. Add carrots and liquid. Bring to a boil, then reduce the heat to simmer. Simmer 2 hours or until the meat is fork tender. Check after the first hour and add more water or beer as needed. Garnish with chopped parsley. Serve with buttered, boiled potatoes.

Note: Texans may want to use a Texas beer instead of Guinness. The flavor may vary slightly.

Pot on the Fire

The thrifty Irish immigrants made this with the leftover gravy from the stew.

Leftover gravy
Milk to stretch the recipe
Sour cream
Herbs to taste

Put the gravy and milk in a food processor or blender. Blend about 30 seconds until smooth. Heat. Pour into a bowl and serve with a dab of sour cream and a sprinkle of fresh herbs.

Soda Bread

2   cups flour

2   teaspoons double-acting baking
    powder

1   teaspoon salt

1   tablespoon sugar

3   tablespoons shortening

⅔   cup milk plus ⅓ cup milk (if needed)

1   cup raisins

Mix the flour, baking powder, salt, and sugar. Cut in the shortening. Quickly pour in ⅔ cup of milk and stir. Slowly add only enough more milk to make dough. Fold in the raisins. Knead lightly about 20 times. Pat the dough into a smooth, dome-shaped loaf. Place on a well-greased cookie sheet. Bake at 350° for 25 minutes. Increase heat to 400° and bake for an additional 5 minutes.

Shepherd's Pie

2   pounds lean ground beef

1   cup diced onion

1   cup diced carrots

1   cup diced celery

1½ cups corn (fresh, frozen or
    canned—drained)

2   cloves minced garlic

½   teaspoon salt

¼   teaspoon pepper

½   teaspoon nutmeg

1   cup beef broth

1   tablespoon melted butter mixed with
    2 tablespoons flour

3   cups mashed potatoes

¼   cup melted butter or margarine

Brown ground beef in large skillet. Add onion, carrots, celery, garlic, and seasonings. Lower heat and cook for about 10 minutes until the vegetables are wilted. Add beef broth and bring to a boil. Stir in the butter/flour mixture to make a thick gravy. Pour mixture into a large, shallow baking pan and cool.

Cover the meat mixture with the corn and then top with hot mashed potatoes. Smooth the mashed potatoes evenly over the filling. Brush surface with melted butter. Bake at 325° for 35-40 minutes.

Baby Carrots and Onions in Cream

1 pound baby carrots
1 pound small white onions
½ cup cream
½ teaspoon salt
¼ teaspoon pepper
¼ teaspoon nutmeg

Wash the carrots and peel the onions. Place in a pot with about ½ inch of water. Cover and simmer gently for 10 minutes. Remove the lid and continue cooking over low heat until the water is absorbed. Shake the pan occasionally to keep the vegetables from burning. Stir in the cream. Add the salt, pepper, and nutmeg, adjusting the amounts to taste. Heat slowly until warm. Do not boil. Put in serving dish and dust lightly with nutmeg. Serve warm.

Note: Use either fresh or frozen carrots and onions.

Milk does not work as well as cream in this recipe; however, sour cream is great!

Dark Irish Soda Bread

3 cups white flour
2 cups whole-wheat flour
2 teaspoons baking soda
1 tablespoon baking powder
2 tablespoons brown sugar
2¼ cups buttermilk
½ cup bran

Mix all dry ingredients together in a large bowl. Pour in the buttermilk and stir until a soft dough forms. Knead on a lightly floured board for a minute or two. Divide the dough in half. Shape each half into a round loaf about 2 inches thick. Pat the top down and dust with flour. Place the loaves on a large ungreased baking sheet. (Use nonstick sheet or spray lightly with cooking spray.) Cut a deep cross with a sharp knife on the tops. Bake at 400° for about 45 minutes. The soda bread is done when it sounds hollow when you knock on the top. Rub the crust with butter or margarine as soon as you take it out of the oven.

Irish Eggs

In English pubs these are called Scotch eggs. Whatever you call them, they are a tasty and easy-to-make snack or light meal.

5   hard-boiled eggs
1   pound bulk sausage meat
1   egg
1   tablespoon milk
1   cup bread crumbs
Paprika and mustard for garnish, if desired

Peel the hard-boiled eggs. Wrap sausage meat completely around each egg. Lightly beat the raw egg and milk. Dip each sausage-covered egg into the milk mixture, then roll in bread crumbs. Place on a broiling rack in a pan. Bake at 350° for one hour. When cool, cut each egg into quarters. Garnish with a dab of your favorite mustard and sprinkle with paprika.

Note: The Irish eggs can be assembled ahead of time. Bring to room temperature before baking. Reheat the leftovers in the microwave for a quick, nourishing breakfast.

Spiced Beef

Spiced Beef is an Irish Christmas tradition. Smelling it cook all day puts everyone in a festive mood!

7-8 pounds beef brisket
2   teaspoons cloves
2   teaspoons mace
2   teaspoons allspice
2   teaspoons cinnamon
2   teaspoons thyme
2   teaspoons pepper
2   tablespoons brown sugar
2   tablespoons molasses
2   tablespoons salt
1   bottle Guinness

Mix together all the ingredients except the beef and Guinness. Rub the seasonings into the beef, cover, and refrigerate. Once or twice a day rub the seasonings into the meat for a week. Put the meat in a large Dutch oven and cover with water. Add the beer and simmer gently for 5-6 hours. Let the meat cool after it is done. Press the meat between two plates with a weight on top. Slice across the grain. Serve warm or cold.

Note: A true Irishman will only want Guinness in this recipe, but for the rest of us, any beer will do. This can also be baked in the oven at 250° until tender, about 5-6 hours.

Trifle

The English, Irish, and Scots all claim trifle. It is delicious, regardless of who originated it!

1   sponge cake, pound cake, or package of ladyfingers

¼   cup sherry (optional)

½   cup raspberry or strawberry jam

2-4   cups fresh or frozen fruit (strawberries, raspberries, peaches, bananas, etc.)

2   packages (5½ oz.) instant vanilla pudding

4   cups milk

Whipping cream and fresh fruit for garnish

Mix the pudding with the milk, following package directions. Place slices of cake on the bottom of a glass bowl. Sprinkle with sherry. Spread the cake with jam. Cover with a layer of pudding and then a layer of fruit. Repeat the layers: cake, sherry, jam, pudding, then fruit. Repeat the layers until you reach the top of the bowl. Refrigerate. Before serving, top with whipped cream and garnish with fresh fruit.

Note: This is a beautiful dessert to make in a clear glass bowl so the different layers show. There is a lot of room for individualization in this recipe!

Although the sherry is optional, I highly recommend it!

Dublin Sheet Cake

Decadently rich!

2 cups flour
1 tablespoon cinnamon
2 teaspoons baking soda
2 cups sugar
2 sticks (16 tablespoons) butter or margarine
2 tablespoons cocoa
1 cup water
2 eggs
½ cup buttermilk

Bring the butter, cocoa, and water to a rolling boil. Mix in the dry ingredients. Add the eggs and buttermilk. Beat well. Pour into a greased and floured (or sprayed) jellyroll pan. Bake at 350° for 20-25 minutes.

Topping: (make while cake is baking)

1 stick (8 tablespoons) butter or margarine
4 tablespoons cocoa
6 tablespoons buttermilk
1 teaspoon vanilla
1 box (1 pound) powdered sugar
1¼ cups chopped nuts

Boil together the butter and cocoa. Remove from heat. Add the remaining ingredients and beat until blended. Spread over the hot cake.

Tri-Colour

This is a patriotic drink of the three colors in the Irish flag!

1 tablespoon crème de menthe
1 tablespoon Bailey's Irish Crème Liqueur
1 teaspoon brandy

Pour the crème de menthe into a liqueur glass. Float Bailey's very slowly on top. Float brandy VERY slowly on top of the Bailey's.

Note: Toast Slainte! and drink slowly so that you taste the crème de menthe last.

Irish Coffee

Here is the traditional toast when drinking Irish coffee:

Health and long life to you,
Land without rent to you,
The woman of your choice to you,
A child every year to you,
A long life, and may your
Bones rest in Ireland.

1½ teaspoons sugar
¾ cup hot black coffee
1   jigger Irish whiskey
2   tablespoons whipped cream

Heat a stemmed whiskey goblet. Add the sugar and coffee. Add the whiskey to within an inch of the brim. Spoon the whipped cream on top, but do not stir. The hot whiskey/coffee is sipped through the whipped cream.

Note: If you don't have a stemmed whiskey goblet, any glass coffee mug will do—but the prettier, the better!

Sauerkraut and Sausages—

The Germans in Texas

Bratwurst, knockwurst, wienerwurst
Herrings in sour cream sauce
Cucumber salad
Potato salad
Dill, sour, and other assorted pickles
Rye and pumpernickel bread
Hard-boiled eggs
Assorted mustards
And much, much more…

This is a typical Christmas Eve supper for Jenny Davis's family as well as for many other families of German descent in Texas. Feasting continues into Christmas Day when all the relatives enjoy a roast goose or turkey stuffed with a kraut and caraway dressing. Families of German descent keep their heritage alive in the wonderful foods they eat for regular meals, but especially during holidays.

German migration to Texas was jump-started in the 1840s when a group of noblemen formed a society to settle Germans in Texas on land they had bought. To entice Germans to resettle, the *Verein* promised furnished houses, farm implements, and financial help until the first crop came in. In addition they promised to help establish schools and churches. The *Verein*'s motivation was partly philanthropic—to help the German peasants who sought a better life—but it was also economic. They hoped to find new sources of raw materials and possibly establish political influence in the independent Republic of Texas. Unfortunately, the *Verein* was poorly organized and underfunded so it was not able to fulfill its promises to the disillusioned settlers who had trusted them.

They did, however, secure claim to a three-million-acre tract of land in the San Antonio-Austin area where a large number of Germans eventually did settle. This is evident in the names of towns in that area: New Braunfels, Fredericksburg, Pflugerville, and Boerne, among many others. To facilitate the movement of settlers from the coast to the interior, German immigrants formed the seaport of Karlshaven, which was much closer to San Antonio than Galveston. The seaport's name was changed to Indianola and became an important military depot. An experiment using camels as beasts of burden to move cargo ended when the town was destroyed by the first of two hurricanes in 1875. A second hurricane eleven years later caused a tidal wave that destroyed the rebuilt city. Though once a bustling seaport, Indianola died after the second devastating hurricane.

Fortunately, the German immigrants fared better. With the promised support from the *Verein* not forthcoming, the people banded together as they had in the old country. They soon discovered that the land was more appropriate for grazing than for farming. To thwart cattle rustlers (a serious problem in the 1870s) they formed the Germania Farmer Verein, possibly the oldest farmers' cooperative in Texas. Members branded their cattle with a "G" on its left shoulder in addition to their own brands. That additional brand warned cattle rustlers that they would enrage the wrath of the entire group and most likely be caught and punished. The cooperative is still active today. Since cattle rustling is no longer the problem it once was, the *Verein* now provides other types of useful services of benefit to its members.

Germany in the middle of the 1800s was not a unified nation as it is now, but rather an assortment of provinces and duchies. People were of different religions—predominantly Catholic and Lutheran. Those who left came to Texas for many different reasons. Some came to escape religious persecution and others to escape starvation and economic hardships. Many of the immigrants were artisans and professionals. Several groups were neither, but rather academic "free thinkers" who attempted to establish several "Latin Settlements," or utopian societies. None of these survived, perhaps because these idealists did not realize the hard physical work necessary just to survive. Philosophizing and pondering truths of the universe did not put food on the table.

Wherever the Germans settled, other groups joined them. The Wends, Czechs, and Poles all sought land near the German settlements. All these groups lived in close proximity to each other in Europe. The continuously changing boundaries in Europe meant that at different times the Germans governed some or all of these groups. The result was an intermingling of cultures. Many of their foods and traditions are very similar. Since many of these peoples were escaping German persecution in Europe when they came to Texas, it is ironic that they chose to live near them here. Eventually these people adopted

many of the German customs, and some, like the Wends, even eventually adopted the German language. (One of the reasons the Wends left their part of Germany was to preserve their own language!) In 1850 about five percent of the population in Texas claimed German blood. Today the percentage is almost four times that, making Germans the fourth largest ethnic group in the state.

The Germans originally brought many of the traditions that Texans of all ethnic backgrounds follow here. Every year on Thanksgiving afternoon after my family has consumed enough food to feed a starving third-world village, we carry on a German tradition: We decorate gingerbread houses. Just as the Germans once did, we bake the gingerbread at least a week in advance to allow it to harden before constructing a fragrant house laden with candy and rock-hard icing. The gingerbread houses mark the beginning of the Christmas season. Then, beginning on December first, we open a door a day on an Advent calendar. Like many Americans everywhere, my family considers these traditions, brought by the Germans to Texas, a normal part of our holiday celebration.

On St. Nicholas Day, December 6, German children put out their shoes so the good saint can leave them a special treat during the night. Many Texas children still do this, except they are more likely to put out a cowboy boot than a shoe!

The first public Christmas tree in Texas was an oak tree decorated with candles in the coastal town of Port Lavaca in 1844 by a German Protestant minister. Hill Country Germans substituted cedar or juniper trees, because those grew in the area. Wherever they were, German parents decorated their trees with whatever they had—bits of colored paper, ribbons, decorated cookies, and candies among other things. The children did not see the tree until Christmas Eve, but even from the closed parlor doors they could smell the delightful aroma of the highly polished oranges and apples hanging on the tree. These delicacies were only available at Christmastime. Candles provided illumination, giving the tree a fantasy glow that seemed almost magical to the children. However, candles also presented a serious fire hazard. Buckets of sand or water always stood near the tree. The men or older boys armed with sponges on long sticks, snuffed out any candle that burned too low before it could set the tree ablaze.

To reduce the fire hazard of the trees, the Germans, like other early settlers, put the tree up as close to Christmas as possible. However, they kept the tree in their homes until the Epiphany, January 6. Many families still follow this custom.

Today, of course, everyone and not just the Germans have beautifully decorated Christmas trees. When inexpensive manufactured ornaments became available at the beginning of the twentieth century, these replaced the homemade ones of the past.

The German settlers also introduced their Advent wreath. Each candle was a different color and had a different meaning. Today the candles in the Advent wreath are often all the same color, but each one still carries a different meaning. Germans also placed a lighted candle in a window so the Christ Child would know He was welcome to enter. Many people still place lights in their windows at Christmas, even if they no longer know where this custom originated.

Kris Kringle comes from *Christkindlein*, the German word for Christ Child. Today we use St. Nicholas, Santa Claus, and Kris Kringle almost interchangeably. Kris Kringle is thought to have been started by Martin Luther, who wanted children to believe that the Christ Child brought them gifts; however, the idea of a separate entity being the gift-giver was too well established. The German Kris Kringle is dressed in long bishop's robes, rather than in a bright red suit. To children, he was a stern judge of their behavior. On Christmas Eve, a neighbor or friend dressed as St. Nicholas came to each house. The children were questioned about their behavior and then required to pray with the stern visitor who left each good child an apple or an orange. Frequently, more than one came to a house. Each time, the whole scenario was repeated, including the prayer and the gift of fruit or candy.

The Germans, creating a tradition for all to enjoy today, first brought Christmas cards to Texas. Germans wrote many of the Christmas carols we sing today. "*Stille Nacht, Heilige Nacht*" and "*O Tannenbaum*" are the universally loved "Silent Night, Holy Night" and "O Christmas Tree."

The second day of Christmas, December 26, was a day when the German settlers in Texas enjoyed dances and public parties. Oompah bands played schottisches, waltzes, and polkas for dancing and entertainment. Sometimes the German settlers celebrated Second Christmas on the Sunday after Christmas, just so the good times and revelry could continue a few days longer.

Children were told that the brilliant autumn sunsets in Texas were actually the angels baking cookies for Christmas. That is a sign the German women need to begin their Christmas baking. Some of the wonderful cookies they made were used to decorate the tree, but most were saved for the rounds of entertaining during this festive season. An invitation to "come to our tree" was really an invitation to visit and enjoy refreshments. To be prepared, the women made goodies they grew up with in Germany, substituting Texas ingredients for the items they could not get here. So where they had once used

walnuts, they now used the indigenous pecans that grew everywhere. Instead of baking a traditional German goose, they enjoyed one of the plentiful wild Texas turkeys.

One German immigrant, August Weidmann, began a bakery in Corsicanna at the end of the nineteenth century. Using a recipe he brought with him, the bakery made and still makes *weiss kuchen mit frucht,* better known to us today as DeLuxe Fruitcakes. Every year thousands of orders are received from around the world for this delicious Christmas treat.

When the German colonists first came to the Fredericksburg area, they invaded the land of the Comanches who were understandably hostile to the newcomers they viewed as interlopers. A German, John Meusebach, negotiated a treaty with the Indians. During the talks, the Indians signaled each other by building fires in the hills surrounding the town. The fires frightened the children until a lady explained to them that the Easter bunny needed the fires to boil all the eggs for Easter eggs! Since Easter was not for

another month, that poor bunny must have been coloring a lot of eggs! However, the lighting of fires around a village is a custom that dates to pagan times in Germany. Unwittingly, an old German custom was revived in Texas. Even today, fires are lit around the town of Fredericksburg at Easter time to commemorate this story.

The German influence is still strongly felt in the Hill Country area around Fredericksburg and other areas where they settled. One of the most popular German celebrations each year is Octoberfest. Although the original settlers may not have had the huge parties that are common today, the idea of celebrating the harvest and the new beer came from Germany. All ethnic groups today celebrate Octoberfest because it is a time of great fun for everyone, not just the Germans.

Eating well was, and still is, a hallmark of German hospitality. Traditional favorites still have their place on holiday and everyday menus.

German Recipes

Grace After Meals

Danket dem Herrn denn er ist Freundlich
Und seine Gnade and Gute wahret Ewiglich. Amen

Thank the Lord for He is kind
His mercy and goodness endure forever. Amen

Biersuppe
(Beer Soup)

One of my tasters considered this a "comfort food." The milk base makes this soup mild and smooth and very soothing.

1   cup milk
1   stick cinnamon
1   tablespoon brown sugar
2   teaspoons cornstarch
1   can (12 oz.) beer
1   egg yolk

Optional garnishes:
  grated cheddar cheese
  crisp bacon bits
  chopped chives
  parsley sprigs
  chopped cilantro (for a Mexican touch)
  a spoonful of your favorite salsa

Boil the milk and cinnamon stick. Reduce heat. Mix sugar, cornstarch, and egg yolk. Mix a little of the hot milk into the egg mixture. Stir the egg mixture into the milk. Cook over low heat, stirring constantly, until thickened. Add the beer and reheat without boiling. Garnish as desired. Serve hot or cold.

Note: Try white sugar in this recipe for a slightly milder flavor.

Senf Eier
(Mustard Eggs)

This is an easy change from deviled eggs.

6   warm, hard-boiled eggs
1   tablespoon of your favorite mustard
4   tablespoons butter or margarine
¼   cup bread crumbs

Peel the eggs and cut in half lengthwise. Put a dab (or more, depending on your taste) of mustard on each egg yolk. Melt butter and drizzle over eggs. Sprinkle with bread crumbs. Serve warm.

Note: Change the type of mustard to add variety to these eggs.

Arme Ritter
("Poor Knight Fritters")

This is not ordinary French toast!

¾   cup milk
2   eggs
1   tablespoon sugar
1   teaspoon vanilla
½   teaspoon grated lemon rind
6   or more slices bread
¾   cup bread crumbs
2   tablespoons butter or margarine

Beat eggs and milk in a pie plate. Add sugar, vanilla, and lemon rind. Dip bread in the egg mixture, then in the dry bread crumbs. Brown in butter.

Serve warm sprinkled with cinnamon sugar, powdered sugar, or syrup.

Note: For a special treat, trim the crusts off the bread and cut each slice into halves or thirds. This makes small, elegant fritters.

Bratwurst Mit Sauer Rahmsosse
(Steamed Bratwurst in Sour Cream Sauce)

8   bratwurst sausages
2   tablespoons butter or margarine
¼   cup cold water
1   tablespoon flour
¼   teaspoon salt
1   cup sour cream

Boil 2 quarts of water and drop in the bratwurst. Remove from the heat, but let the bratwurst soak for 5 minutes. Drain and pat dry. Melt the butter in a large skillet and brown the bratwurst. Add ¼ cup cold water to the skillet; reduce heat and simmer uncovered 10 minutes. Turn the bratwurst over, using tongs. Simmer another 10 minutes. Add a little more water if needed. Remove the bratwurst from the pan. Mix together the flour, salt, and sour cream. Add a few tablespoons at a time to the liquid remaining in the skillet. Cook over low heat, stirring constantly until sauce is smooth and slightly thickened. **Do not let the sour cream sauce boil.** Slice the bratwurst into ¼ inch rounds. Drop them in the skillet and baste with the sauce. Simmer only long enough to heat the bratwurst thoroughly.

Wiener Schnitzel

1½ pounds veal cutlets, pounded very thin
¾ cup flour
2   eggs, beaten slightly
1   cup very fine bread crumbs
¾ cup butter or margarine
¼ teaspoon salt
⅛ teaspoon pepper
Lemon slices
Anchovy fillets (optional)

Season the flour with the salt and pepper. Dip the meat into the seasoned flour, then egg, then bread crumbs. Sauté the schnitzels in the melted butter over low heat until golden brown on both sides, approximately 15 minutes. Keep the schnitzels warm in a very low oven. To serve, garnish with thin lemon slices topped with an anchovy fillet.

Note: Boned chicken breast pounded very thin can be used instead of veal.

For a little variety, try any of the seasoned bread crumbs in your grocery store, or make your own. In an emergency make crumbs in the food processor from any unsweetened breakfast cereal you have on hand.

Wiener Schnitzel a La Holstein

wiener schnitzel
1   fried egg for each piece of schnitzel

Make wiener schnitzel using the preceding recipe. Top each schnitzel with a fried egg. Garnish with anchovy fillets and lemon slices.

Rabbit Stew

Every cook had her own special recipe for rabbit stew. Rabbits were every-where. Fortunately, this cute but pesky animal makes for good eating! Similar cooking techniques were also used with squirrels.

1   rabbit, preferably young and tender
1   teaspoon salt
1   teaspoon pepper
2   tablespoons flour (more if the rabbit is large)
4   tablespoons oil or shortening
⅔   cup water

Cut the rabbit into individual serving-size pieces. Roll each piece in a mixture of the flour, salt, and pepper. Heat the fat in a large pot or skillet. Brown the rabbit pieces on all sides. Add the water, cover, and simmer until tender, about 1½ hours.

Note: Potatoes, carrots, or other vegetables can be added if you want to cook the entire meal in one pot. Add your own seasonings to make this uniquely yours. This also works well in a slow cooker.

New Peas with Onions and Herbs

1   package (16 oz.) frozen peas
6   green onions
¼   teaspoon pepper
1   tablespoon sugar
2   tablespoons butter or margarine
1   teaspoon flour
½   cup boiling water
1   tablespoon herbs (any combination of parsley, tarragon, chives, and chervil)

Slice the white part of the green onions in ½ inch lengths. Combine the onions and peas in a small pan. Add pepper and sugar. Melt butter and stir in the flour. Slowly add the water, stirring constantly. Cover and cook until peas are heated. Stir herbs into peas.

Potato Bake

This is an easy side dish to bake in the oven with whatever else is being cooked.

3   potatoes, peeled and thinly sliced
1   onion, thinly sliced
3   tomatoes, sliced
4   slices of bacon cut into 1" pieces
½ cup shredded cheese (more if desired)
Dash of pepper

Grease or spray a casserole dish. Place a layer of potatoes on the bottom of the dish and gently pepper. Cover with a layer of onion slices, then tomatoes, then bacon. Repeat in the same order until the dish is filled. Finish with bacon on the top. Sprinkle with cheese. Cover and bake at 350° until the potatoes are soft, about 45 minutes to an hour.

Note: Roma tomatoes are good in this recipe. But because they are small, you may need to use four or more.

Sweet Rice

My husband has vivid memories of his German grandmother fixing sweet rice for him and serving it with fried chicken! Even though this is very sweet, it is NOT dessert.

1   cup rice
2¼ cups milk
2   cups water
4   tablespoons butter or margarine
1   teaspoon salt
½ teaspoon cinnamon
⅓ cup sugar

Boil the rice and the water. Add the milk and salt. Simmer in a covered pan, stirring so the rice does not stick. Add extra milk if the rice is not tender when the mixture has reached a creamy texture. Transfer to an ovenproof dish. Stir in the cinnamon and sugar. Melt the butter and pour it over the rice. Keep warm in the oven until ready to serve.

German Potato Salad

Each region of Germany has its own version of potato salad, and each cook has her own special variations. This recipe is the one Jenny Davis's mother likes to make. It is just one of many variations.

Yukon gold potatoes
Light vegetable oil
Balsamic vinegar
Chopped onion
Crisp bacon
Bottled Italian salad dressing

Boil the potatoes with the skins still on until they are done, but still firm. Drain and cool to room temperature, then cut into cubes. Lightly mix the potatoes with the oil and vinegar. Sprinkle the potatoes with the chopped onion and crumbled bacon. Toss with bottled Italian dressing.

Note: Proportions vary according to personal tastes and the number of people who will be eating! Many ethnic cooks tend to adjust their cooking each time they prepare a particular dish.

This potato salad will stay fresh in the refrigerator for several days.

Bierocks

1 pound hamburger
1½ cups shredded cabbage
¼ cup finely chopped onion
2 loaves (1 pound each) frozen bread dough, defrosted.

Sauté hamburger, cabbage, and onion until all are cooked. Drain. Roll out one loaf of bread dough until it is about ¼ inch thick. Cut into 4-inch squares. Place a small amount of the meat mixture in the center of each square. Bring the 4 corners together and pinch the ends together. Place the bierocks, pinched side down, on a greased baking sheet. Let rise until doubled in size. Bake at 350° for 20 minutes.

Note: The bread dough can be brushed with egg whites mixed with a little water for a shiny appearance, if desired.

Serve with your favorite German mustard for a tasty snack.

Rindfleisch-Rouladen
(Beef Rolled Meat)

1 tenderized round steak
3 tablespoons butter or margarine
¾ cup bread crumbs
1 onion, diced
2 slices bacon, cut into pieces
1 cup sour cream

Cut the round steak into long strips, one strip per serving. Sauté the bread crumbs, onion, and bacon. Spread evenly on each strip of steak. Roll and fasten with either string or toothpicks. Brown the meat rolls in the butter, turning frequently for even browning. Add water, cover, and simmer for 2 hours. Test for tenderness with a fork. Fifteen minutes before serving, remove the meat rolls from the pan. Stir in the sour cream and simmer until warm. Pour over the meat rolls.

Blitz Kaffee Kuchen
(Quick Coffee Cake)

This fast, easy coffee cake is perfect for breakfast or afternoon coffee.

4 tablespoons butter or margarine
½ cup sugar
1 egg
⅔ cup milk
2 teaspoons baking powder
¼ teaspoon salt
½ teaspoon nutmeg
2 cups flour

Topping:
½ cup sugar
1 teaspoon cinnamon

Cream together the butter and sugar. Add egg and beat well. Add dry ingredients alternately with the milk. Pour into greased (or sprayed with cooking spray) cake pan—the smaller the pan, the thicker the cake. Mix together the sugar and cinnamon for the topping. Sprinkle over the top of the cake. Bake at 350° for about 30 minutes or until a toothpick inserted in the center comes out clean.

Christmas Cake

Just smelling this cake bake will put even the grumpiest Scrooge in the Christmas spirit!

½ cup butter or margarine
2 cups sugar
3 eggs
1 jar (4 oz.) strained prunes (baby food)
1 teaspoon baking soda
2 cups flour
1 teaspoon nutmeg
1 teaspoon cloves
1 teaspoon cinnamon
1 cup buttermilk
1 cup chopped pecans (optional)

Cream together the butter and sugar. Add eggs, one at a time, beating well after each addition. Add the strained prunes. Beat well. Add the dry ingredients alternately with the buttermilk, beating well after each addition. Stir in the pecans last. Pour into a greased and floured bundt pan (or sprayed). Bake at 350° for 60 minutes.

Note: This cake can be baked in any type of pan; just adjust the cooking time accordingly. It makes wonderful gifts when baked in miniature loaf pans or even in clean, round vegetable cans!

Try spreading a slice of Christmas cake with cream cheese and sprinkling with cinnamon—delicious!

This is a moist, heavy cake that stays fresh for a long time. It also freezes beautifully.

Sauerkraut Cake

Do not tell anyone what kind of cake this is until after they have tried it.
They will love it, even if they do not like sauerkraut!

⅔ cup butter

1½ cups sugar

1 tablespoon vanilla

3 eggs

2½ cups flour

½ cup cocoa

1 teaspoon soda

1 teaspoon baking powder

¼ teaspoon salt

1 cup water

⅔ cup sauerkraut, drained and finely chopped

Cream together butter, sugar, and vanilla. Add eggs one at a time, beating well. Combine the dry ingredients. Add the dry ingredients to the butter mixture, alternating with the water. When well mixed, stir in the sauerkraut. Grease and flour or spray a 9" x 13" cake pan. Bake at 350° for 30 minutes.

Note: If you are short on time, chop the drained sauerkraut in a food processor and add to your favorite chocolate cake mix. Either way, it is a delicious, very moist cake that will keep for several days.

Black Forest Cake

This cake is a favorite!

3   round layers of your favorite dark chocolate cake

⅓   cup grape or raspberry jelly

3   tablespoons cherry liqueur (optional)

½   can cherry pie filling

1   cup whipping cream

Chocolate curls for garnish

Chocolate icing or additional whipped cream

Sprinkle the cherry liqueur over the first layer of cake. Spread the jelly over the first layer. Spread the cherry pie filling over the jelly, reserving a few perfectly formed cherries. Rinse and dry the reserved cherries. Place the second cake layer on top of the first. Whip the cream, but do not add sugar. Spread the whipped cream over the second layer. Top with the last layer. Frost with chocolate icing or additional whipped cream. Decorate with chocolate curls and the reserved cherries.

Note: Use a mix or make the cake from scratch—the choice is yours.

Chocolate curls are easy to make— just "peel" a strip of chocolate from a block of chocolate with a potato peeler!

Torte

This is an extremely easy dessert to make, but it tastes like you labored for days!

- 4 frozen pie shells for 9-inch deep-dish pies (or more)
- 1 jar (10 oz. or larger) raspberry jelly
- 1 tablespoon sherry (optional)

Defrost the frozen pie pastry. Roll the pastry thin and put on the bottom of an inverted pie plate. Cut off any extra pastry so you have a flat circle of pastry. Prick with a fork in several places. Bake at 450° for 3-4 minutes until light brown. Beat the jelly with a fork for smoother spreading. Stir in the sherry, if desired. Place the first layer on a serving plate and spread the jelly generously between the layers as they come out of the oven. On the top layer, dust with powdered sugar rather than jelly. The torte should ripen (age) at least 2 or 3 days before serving. It does not need to be refrigerated.

Note: You need between 12 and 20 layers for this torte. If you want to make each layer bigger in diameter than the bottom of the pie plates that the pastry comes in, you will need more packages of frozen pie pastries.

Of course, you can use your own favorite pastry recipe rather than use the frozen ones!

Melasses Plätzchen
(Molasses Cookies)

2   cups flour
2   teaspoons baking soda
¼   teaspoon salt
1   teaspoon cinnamon
¾   teaspoon ground cloves
¾   teaspoon ginger
¾   cup shortening
1   cup sugar
1   egg
¼   cup molasses
½   cup powdered sugar (optional)

Mix together the flour, baking soda, salt, and spices. Add the remaining ingredients and beat well. (You may need to use your hands for the last bit of mixing.) Shape into small balls and place on a greased or sprayed cookie sheet. Press with a fork, like for peanut butter cookies. Bake at 350° for 10 minutes. When done, remove to a cooling rack. Sift powdered sugar over the warm cookies, if desired.

Poles Under the Oak—

The Polish in Texas

Saturday, July 11, 1998, was not an ordinary weekend day in Panna Maria, Texas, about an hour's drive south of San Antonio. Though visitors occasionally come to this rural community, the special guest on this day was not an ordinary tourist. The guest of honor was the Prime Minister of Poland, Jerzy Buzek, who had just met with President Clinton in Washington, D.C., to discuss NATO concerns. Before returning to Poland, the prime minister planted a tree near the site where the first Polish immigrants to Texas had celebrated their first mass. Buzek felt a certain kinship with the residents of this small town because he, like the original settlers of Panna Maria, was from Silesia, an area in the south of Poland. And like the locals, he left the ceremony wearing a cowboy hat and boots.

Poland ceased to exist at the end of the eighteenth century. What had once been an independent country was divided among Germany, Austria, and Russia. As a result, many of the Polish traditions brought to Texas actually originated in one of these other areas. Living conditions, which were meager even before the dissolution of Poland, declined regardless of whose rule they fell under. Life was particularly hard under the Germans. The Polish people were systematically deprived of their land, forbidden to speak their native language, and were generally discriminated against. Adding poverty to this mix of hardships made the Poles acutely interested in the glowing reports they were hearing about Texas. Texas seemed to be the golden land of opportunity where labor was scarce and land was plentiful.

When Father Leopold Moczygemba from the Upper Prussian Silesia area wrote to his family and friends that he had found a location for a Polish settlement in Texas, one hundred families sold all their belongings so they could make the trip. After nine weeks of sailing over rough seas, the group finally landed in Galveston. Plague and yellow fever greeted them. Some were too sick or despondent to continue to the land Father Leopold had chosen for them. They settled in the nearest community when they could no longer go on. Those healthy enough to continue, did. They proceeded on their three-week overland trek to an area about fifty-five miles south of San Antonio. They arrived at their final destination on Christmas Eve, 1854. This night, called *Wigilia* (from the Latin meaning "to watch"), is the most important holiday of the year for Catholic Poles. At midnight they gathered for the traditional Shepherd's Mass under the largest oak tree in sight. In front of a makeshift altar that Father Leopold had made, they not only celebrated a mass of thanksgiving for their safe arrival, but they also asked for the strength to continue on what seemed to be an impossible task before them. Then they sang traditional Polish Christmas carols.

The new settlement was named Panna Maria for the Virgin Mary in honor of the day they arrived. The oak tree still stands today. Nearby is the Immaculate Conception Church these hearty people established. Father Leopold was buried in front of this church. And this is where the prime minister planted a tree and spoke to these descendants of the original colonists.

During that first night and the cold, rainy days that followed, the people slept in shallow holes they had dug in the ground for warmth and shelter. During the next few years they endured many discouraging hardships while trying to tame the vast Texas prairie. Gradually the conditions changed in Panna Maria, the oldest Polish settlement not only in Texas, but also in the United States.

Since World War II, Texas has experienced a second wave of Polish immigration. This group is quite different from the first group that arrived in 1854. Today's newcomers tend to be well-educated professionals who settle in cities, whereas those who arrived a century and a half ago came to escape poverty and discrimination in Europe.

Many of the descendants of the original group of settlers still live in Panna Maria as successful farmers of the land their ancestors originally tilled. And Christmas in Panna Maria, Bremond, and other areas where Polish people live in Texas, is still celebrated in a manner similar to the way it was celebrated by the people who survived that first difficult Christmas Eve in Texas.

Preparations for Christmas begin early in December when cooks begin preparing traditional foods such as *piernik*, a honey spice cake. These little cakes were popularized by an order of St. Catherine nuns, so this treat is now known as Little Catherines. *Piernik* are still sometimes given as gifts on Saint Nicholas Day on December 6. Small presents or sweets may also be given to

good children on this day, but today the idea of Santa Claus delays gift-giving until Christmas Eve.

A number of superstitions about Christmas Eve are still enjoyed, even if they are not actually believed. Many of these superstitions date back to the era when December 24 was considered the last day of the year. Events that happened on Christmas Eve were then considered to be predictions of what would happen in the coming year. Most of these had to do with health, wealth, marriage, and status. For example, a sneeze during this day signified good health in the coming year, and a sunny day guaranteed lots of eggs as well as a marriage for the young and poor. A cloudy day meant a lot of milk and marriage for the old and wealthy. Polishing your teeth with garlic was supposed to bring strength.

Straw is supposed to be placed under the tablecloth for wealth in the New Year. If the straw at an unmarried girl's place is long and green, she will have a speedy marriage. If it is blackened, she will have a long wait, and if it is yellow, she will never marry. One extra plate is always on the table for the spirit of a dead relative or for an unexpected guest.

Christmas Eve supper begins as soon as the first star appears in the sky and never before. If the night is cloudy and the stars are hidden, supper must wait until everyone is sure it is late enough for the stars to be seen, even if they are not visible at the time. One tradition requires that

twelve different dishes be served, one for each apostle. However, other Poles believe that an odd number of dishes—at least seven, but usually nine or thirteen—should be served to ensure a good harvest the next year. The meal begins when the patriarch of the family breaks the *oplatek*, a special wafer that represents, love, friendship, and forgiveness. The *oplatek* is then passed from one person to the next. Each one breaks off a piece and eats it. Traditionally, even the farm animals are given a piece of it to ensure healthy offspring. Typically, the meal will include *pierogi* (a type of filled dumpling), sweet cabbage, peas, and a poppy seed cake or pastry for dessert. Fish will also be served because no meat is eaten on the day of Christmas Eve.

Once the meal begins, no one is to leave the table until it is over. Leaving was believed to bring bad luck or even death in the coming year. Staying seated at the table must have been extremely difficult for excited, restless children who were forced to endure the drudgery of listening to hours of grown-up conversation.

After supper, but before midnight mass, the family might open gifts and sing Christmas songs by the Christmas tree in the parlor. The tree would be decorated with eggs or eggshells to symbolize the miracle of birth, apples to bring beauty and health, and nuts to bring happiness and love. Other decorations would represent stars, angels, or items of nature such as birds or animals. Although these decorations may still adorn a family's tree, typical American decorations are also used now.

The *Pasterka* or Shepherd's Mass at midnight is still celebrated with the same joy and importance that it was on Christmas Eve in 1854 by the first settlers of Panna Maria. After the busy-ness of Christmas Eve, Christmas Day is a day to enjoy being with family. Unlike some holidays, when everyone except the women who spend the day cooking get to relax, even they get to take some time off. No work is supposed to be performed on Christmas Day, even by the women. The meal needs to be something that can be prepared ahead of time. Meat, traditionally some sort of pork such as Polish ham or sausage, is usually eaten.

In Poland, St. Stephen's Day, December 26, was also the day to hire employees for the following year. The hostess would prepare a special meal for all of her domestic workers. Anyone who did not eat was indicating that he was leaving to work someplace else. Eating indicated a commitment to work throughout the coming year. When the Poles came to Texas, they were too poor to hire others to work for them. They intensively farmed smaller plots of land so they did not need to hire help. Also, in Texas they worked for themselves on their own land so there was no question about whether they would be around to work for another year. Of course

they would! In Texas, St. Stephen's Day became a day for prolonging the Christmas spirit by visiting with friends and relatives. Christmas parties and other festivities are traditionally held after Christmas, rather than before. Without the distractions before Christmas, the Polish Catholics could spend the time before preparing and "watching" for the arrival of the Christ Child.

Easter is another important time in the life of the Polish Catholics who came to Texas. Like the Ukrainians who may have influenced them (or perhaps the Poles influenced the Ukrainians, or maybe it originated with the Church), the blessing of the Easter baskets is an important as well as fun ritual. On the day before Easter, beautifully decorated baskets are filled with bits of different types of food that will be eaten at dinner on Easter Sunday. In the baskets are foods such as eggs, horseradish, *kilbuska* (sausage), and pastry. The baskets of food are brought to the church to be blessed by the priest and then taken to the Lord's tomb inside the church. Anyone who has a Polish costume wears it to the church for this ceremony.

Mass is celebrated at dawn on Easter morning. The ritual involves the priest and congregation having a procession around the church. They circle the church three times, signifying the Father, Son, and Holy Ghost.

Polish weddings in Texas tend not to be as elaborate as they are in Poland. If the father of the bride could afford it, the marriage feasting and celebrations sometimes lasted as long as three days in the old country. Wedding receptions in Texas are a lot shorter today. However, certain nuptial characteristics remain the same. Even today, before going to the church for the ceremony, the bridal couple asks both sets of parents for a special blessing. After the blessing from the parents, the mother blesses the couple with holy water. In the past, this blessing was seen as even more important than the church ceremony itself—so important, in fact, that the couple would go to the cemetery on the way to the church to ask a deceased parent (if one had died) for a blessing. Like in the past, today a party with singing, dancing, and abundant food and drink follows the church ceremony. When the couple departed, brides once threw handfuls of straw on the unmarried guests. Whoever it landed on was supposed to get married before the others. Today, like brides throughout the United States, she throws her bouquet to the unmarried females to "foretell" who will be the next one married.

Traditionally, a baby's naming day is considered more important than its birthday. On the naming day, the baby is baptized with the name of the saint whose day it is. Parents take great care in choosing the name of a saint that will bestow special blessings or characteristics on their child. The child is taught about and encouraged to emulate the namesake saint. Even years later, the naming day is celebrated by Polish families, rather than a child's birthday.

Because many of the Polish settlers in Texas settled in close-knit rural communities such as Panna Maria, Bremond, and Chappell Hill, they tended to isolate themselves from outside influences. It is interesting to note that when the Ukrainians came to Texas, they chose to settle near the Polish communities. Having been so close to Poland in Europe, they felt comfortable around them in their new land. Likewise, the Poles had strong cultural connections with the Czechs who lived to the south and the Germans and Wends who lived to the west in Europe.

Some families in Texas maintained Polish as the language spoken in the home for several generations, even though English was used in school and for business. Frequently the priests in these rural towns and in predominantly Polish congregations in the larger cites are from Poland, thus keeping the language, customs, and ties to the old country alive. St. Peter the Apostle Catholic Church in Dallas is led by a priest who is from Poland. The priests learn or improve their English while ministering to their congregation, and the parishioners often learn Polish while maintaining contact with their ethnic roots.

For recent immigrants, first-generation Texans, and those learning Polish from the priest, this sometimes translates into praying and worshipping in the more expressive Polish language even though English is the language used for everything else. Some will even admit to not knowing the English translations to the prayers, but understanding them perfectly in Polish.

Even in the cities where assimilation is the greatest, the Church is making an effort to encourage the keeping of Polish traditions and authenticity. The visit of Prime Minister Jerzy Buzek of Poland to Panna Maria illustrates how close these ties are being maintained.

Polish Recipes

Cwikia
(Beet and Horseradish Relish)

1   can (16 oz.) beets
2   tablespoons horseradish
1   teaspoon sugar

Mix all ingredients in a blender or food processor until coarsely chopped. Cover and let stand in the refrigerator for at least 2 days.

Kluski z Kapusta
(Polish Noodles)

1   package (8 oz.) wide egg noodles

1   stick (8 tablespoons) butter or margarine

5   cloves garlic, minced

1   large onion, chopped

1   large head cabbage, shredded

1   tablespoon caraway seeds

Salt and pepper to taste

1   pint (2 cups) sour cream

Boil the noodles until cooked but still firm. Sauté the garlic, onion, and cabbage in the butter. When the vegetables are limp, add the caraway seeds. Drain noodles. Pour vegetables over the noodles. Mix the sour cream with the noodles and vegetables.

Note: Serve with Polish sausage and a hearty bread such as rye or pumpernickel. Or just serve with bread for a tasty vegetarian meal.

Mizeria
(Cucumbers in Sour Cream)

1   cup peeled and thinly sliced cucumbers

1   teaspoon salt

½   cup sour cream

Juice from ½ lemon

½   teaspoon sugar

1-2 teaspoons minced dill

Mix the salt and cucumbers. Let stand for ten minutes. Drain off the liquid. Mix the sour cream, lemon juice, sugar, and dill. Combine the cucumbers with the sour cream dressing.

Note: Fresh dill is best if you have it. If not, dried dill will do. Adjust the ingredients according to your taste.

Placki Ziemniaczane
(Potato Pancakes)

1½ pounds potatoes

1　onion

1　egg

2　tablespoons flour

Oil for frying

Salt and pepper to taste

1¼ cups sour cream

Peel the potatoes and onion. Grate both finely or use grating disk of the food processor. Lightly beat the egg, add salt and pepper, and add to the grated vegetables. Add enough flour for the mixture to hold its shape. Cover the bottom of a large frying pan with oil. Drop spoonfuls of the potato mixture into the oil. Flatten with a spatula or spoon until very thin. Brown on both sides. Serve warm with sour cream.

Nalesniki
(Crêpes)

Batter:

1   egg
1   egg yolk
1½ cups milk
2   cups flour
Oil for frying

Beat together the egg and egg yolk. Mix in ¾ cup milk, then add the flour. Add the rest of the milk and beat until the batter is smooth. Let it rest for 5 minutes. Heat the oil in the pan and pour the batter into it. Tilt the pan so the batter runs to cover the bottom of the pan and forms a very thin pancake. When brown, turn over and brown the other side. Fill the pancakes with cheese filling or sour cream. Roll them or fold into quarters. Serve warm.

Cheese Filling:

1   cup large curd cottage cheese
1   tablespoon butter or margarine
1   egg yolk
1   teaspoon sugar

Mix all ingredients until smooth (use food processor, mixer, or blender). Heat slowly until warm.

Note: Top with a dab of jelly, honey, or cinnamon and sugar.

Edible Easter Basket

This makes a beautiful, edible centerpiece for Easter. You may be tempted to eat it, or you may decide to freeze it until next year!

3   cups flour

2   packages rapid rise yeast

1   cup milk

4   tablespoons butter or margarine

1   teaspoon sugar

½   teaspoon salt

Butter

2   egg yolks

Combine flour, yeast, salt, and sugar. Scald milk and remove from heat. Add butter and let it melt. Add milk to the flour mixture. Beat well. Form into a ball and let rest for 10 minutes. Roll about ¾ of the dough into a 10-inch square. Cut into 24 strips. Lay out 12 strips and use the other 12 strips to weave between them. Butter the outside of an ovenproof bowl.

Gently place the woven dough over the outside of the bowl. Trim the ends of the dough. Place the dough-covered bowl on a cookie sheet. Brush the strips with the beaten egg yolks. Bake at 350° for 20 minutes. Cover the dough with foil and continue baking for another 25 minutes. Allow the basket to cool on the bowl.

Roll the remaining dough into a rectangle long enough to go around the top edge of the basket. Cut the rectangle into 3 strips and braid. Brush with egg yolk and bake for 20 minutes. Gently remove the basket from the bowl. Attach the warm rim to the basket with toothpicks.

Note: Fill with fruits, vegetables, and decorated eggs.

Flat Paper Chain for the Christmas Tree

This is a fun, easy decoration to make that does not even require glue or paste!

Colored paper

Make a pattern for a circle about 2 ¾" in diameter. Fold a piece of construction paper on the long side of the paper 3" from the edge. Trace around the pattern, making sure that you have one edge of the circle on the fold. Next draw a smaller circle inside the large one, leaving about a ½" strip of paper. Cut out each larger circle, making sure not to cut the folded edge. Fold each cut-out circle in half again and cut out the inner circle. When you open up the cutout you should have a nice round fat figure eight. Fold it back and loop the first cutout through the second one, so that the folded edge catches the second loop. Repeat until the chain is as long as you want, or until you run out of paper!

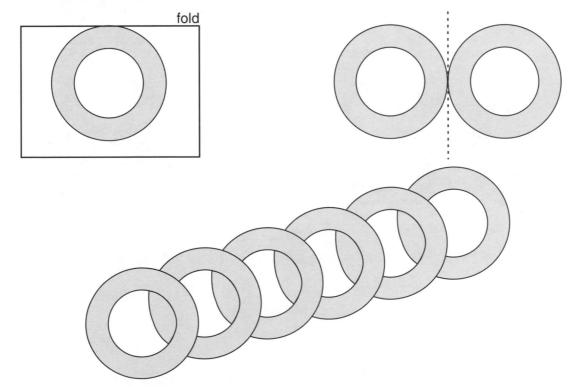

fold

The Search for Freedom—
The Ukrainians in Texas

Saturday night at the AutoNation Community Room in Irving, Texas, may sound like an unusual time and place to celebrate old-world customs. Once a month, a group of Texans of Ukrainian descent meet for a potluck supper and camaraderie. While eating enchiladas and pumpkin pie one November Saturday, this group made plans for an elaborate traditional *Sviata Vechera* or Ukrainian Christmas Eve dinner. However, this *Sviata Vechera* would be held on a Saturday night a few weeks before Christmas rather than on Christmas Eve. This was so the dinner would not interfere with all the other activities associated with a twentieth century Texas Christmas. Different families volunteered to make each of the traditional dishes. Others provided money to cover other expenses of this special night. This spirit of cooperation and the blending of the old and new is how the members of the Ukrainian American Society of Texas

maintain their connection with their roots while living in modern-day Texas.

Over the centuries the Ukrainians have had a lot of practice adapting. Ukraine is strategically located in Eastern Europe between nations frequently at war with one another. This made Ukraine a battleground for other people's wars. She also saw her sons forcibly conscripted into the armies of other nations, thus weakening her own forces. As a result, sections of Ukraine have been under the rule of Poland, the Austrian-Hungarian empire, and Russia. During most of these occupations, Ukraine has been divided into Eastern and Western Ukraine, each being ruled by a different country. In spite of, or maybe because of all these attempts to take over their land, the Ukrainians have had to work all the harder to maintain their own identity. Only in 1991 did Ukraine once again regain its independence after decades of rule by the Soviet Union.

During the Texas Revolution against Mexico in the 1830s, two Ukrainian brothers, Adolph and Frank Petrushewych, well-known military experts of the time, contributed their talents in our fight for freedom. When they came to Texas, they were fleeing the injustices of czarist Russia. The brothers understood the plight of the Texans who were under the rule of another's government.

Other than a few individuals like the Petrushewych brothers, large groups of Ukrainians did not come to Texas until the late 1890s. One group was on its way to Canada when the shipping agents persuaded them to go to Texas instead. When they arrived, they were sorely disappointed in what they found. First, there was no free land to be earned through homesteading. Since they arrived penniless, they could not afford even the low prices being asked for Texas land. Instead, they had to take jobs working on the farms of others or working on the railroad or in the coal mines. They also discovered that there were no established Ukrainian settlements in Texas. Nor were there any Ukrainian churches at that time.

So the Ukrainian immigrants settled in areas where they felt comfortable with the people already there. Since parts of Ukraine had been governed by Poland and many of the Ukrainians already spoke Polish, the first Ukrainian farm settlements were near Polish communities. Settling near Bremond, New Waverly, or Schulenburg helped ease their transition to becoming Texans. Today, of course, Ukrainian groups can be found scattered throughout the state and especially in the large cities such as Dallas, Fort Worth, and Houston.

The church is an extremely important part of Ukrainian life. Although there are other religions, most of the Texas Ukrainians belong to the Catholic or Orthodox churches. Both were incorporated into the Russian Orthodox Church when the country was under Soviet rule. To practice their religion in their own way, the Ukrainians had to do so in secret. If they chose to worship at the state church, they did so knowing that the priests were instruments of the government and therefore required to spy on the parishioners. The priests could and did report sins listed in confession to the government. The freedom to worship in their own churches was one of the appeals of leaving their homeland for the New World.

The Ukrainian Christmas celebration begins thirty-nine days before the event. Advent was considered a solemn time of preparation for the birth of Christ and for fasting. No dancing or marriages were allowed. Instead, this was a time for a thorough cleaning. The women and girls cleaned the house, and the men and boys did the same with the barns and yard. This "spring cleaning" in the

winter played an important secular role, also. It got rid of all the bugs and rodents that, if left undisturbed, would infest the stores of food put up for the long winter. Once those tasks were completed, the females began preparing food for the holy supper on Christmas Eve.

All farm work was to be completed by the Feast of the Presentation on November 21. No work was to be done afterwards for several weeks. So before the feast, the males in the family chopped and stacked enough firewood for the coldest time of the year that was yet to come. To prepare spiritually for the coming holy days, everyone who had quarreled with someone else during the year was expected to make up during this time—a wonderful idea that we could all profit from even today!

By Christmas Eve all the food for the holy supper had been prepared. Hay was placed under the table and under a white or beautifully embroidered tablecloth. A candle was placed in the middle of the *kolach* (a special round loaf of bread). Then the father would bring in a sheaf of the finest grain and place it near the icons on the table. As dusk approached, the family walked around the house three times, representing the Holy Trinity, reciting prayers. After additional prayers inside, the *Sviata Vechera* would be served.

At a *Sviata Vechera* in Texas, just like the ones in Ukraine, twelve dishes are served, and none of them contain meat or dairy products. The first dish is *kutia*, boiled whole wheat with honey and poppy seed. It looks and tastes somewhat like porridge. The remainder of the twelve dishes include family favorites such as *borscht* or pickled mushrooms or beets. Entrees include various types of fish, *pyrohy* (similar to dumplings) with different fillings, potatoes, sauerkraut, or rice. Vegetables may be anything the family likes such as beans, mushrooms, or beets. Dessert is usually a fruit compote or a *pyrohy* with a prune or poppy seed filling. After eating, everyone goes to mass. When they return home, the wonderful cakes and pastries that the women have worked so hard to prepare are served. On Christmas Day, the fast is over and once again meat and dairy products can be eaten.

"The Miracle of the Christmas Tree" is one of the traditional stories told by Ukrainian families. In this tale, the father of a poor family had been conscripted into a foreign army. The mother and children had barely enough to survive, but they still managed to clean the house properly and to prepare a few bites of each of the traditional dishes. They had cut a small tree in the forest and had decorated it with the few stubs of candles that they had left over from the previous year. There was no money to buy colored paper for ornaments or flour to make dough ornaments to hang on the tree. Also living in the house was a little spider that loved the family very much. Feeling sorry for their plight, the spider spent the night of Christmas Eve spinning a glorious web to decorate the tree. In the morning the family rejoiced in its splendor, just as the father came up the walk. He announced that the war was over and that he was home for good. Since that time, a spider living in a house has been considered good luck and no one is to harm it. Today lacy spiderweb ornaments are popular decorations on Christmas trees.

Easter is another time when the Ukrainians have their own special traditions. The blessing of the Easter baskets is an important tradition at this time. Prior to Easter, no one eats any of the wonderful foods that are prepared for this day. Then at the Easter Sunday mass, each person brings an Easter basket filled with a small amount of each of the different foods that will be served at the dinner that follows. The basket is covered with a beautifully decorated cloth called a *rushnyk*. Commonly, the basket will contain butter, salt, *kowbasa* (sausage), and hard-boiled eggs. The priest then blesses each basket of food so that it is ready to eat. The family returns home to enjoy the feast of the food that has been blessed.

Some of the eggs may have been decorated with intricate Ukrainian patterns. The eggshells are decorated with multiple layers of beeswax and different colors of dyes. Decorated Ukrainian Easter eggs are works of art that require much skill and patience to make. The end result is cherished for years. Texans can now buy the ingredients for creating these beautiful eggs, making it possible for this form of folk art to continue.

Icons are an important part of a Ukrainian home. An icon is not prized because of its aesthetic value. Rather it is the representative value of an icon that is important. In fact, the icon is not supposed to be a photographic representation of a religious scene because the beauty may interfere with the religious truth represented by the icon. Beautifully embroidered cloths are often draped over the icons on the wall, connecting them for symbolic meaning.

The Ukrainians, like the other groups who have largely assimilated into mainstream Texans, are struggling to maintain their unique heritage. Meeting in the community room of a car dealership is one way they are striving to do this.

Ukrainian Recipes

The foods that kept the best over the long Ukrainian winters were root vegetables such as carrots, potatoes, and beets. Cabbage was also another staple in their diets. Pickled and dried items such as mushrooms, sauerkraut, pickles, and fruit also provided food in the winter. When the Ukrainians came to Texas, they continued to eat the foods that reminded them of home.

Pickled Mushrooms

2   cans (4 oz. each) mushrooms
1   small onion, thinly sliced
½   cup vinegar
½   cup water
1   bay leaf
5   peppercorns
1   teaspoon salt
1   teaspoon sugar
1   tablespoon oil

In a container with a tight-fitting top, layer the mushrooms and onions. Simmer the vinegar, water, bay leaf, peppercorns, salt, and sugar. Pour this mixture over the mushrooms and onion. Float the oil on top of the mushrooms. Cover tightly. Marinate in the refrigerator for at least 1 to 3 days before serving.

Note: Remove the bay leaf and peppercorns if the flavor starts to become too strong. More vinegar can be added for a sharper taste.

If you are not planning on eating all of the pickled mushrooms within a week or so, pack them in a sterilized canning jar.

Cabbage Borscht

Borscht is a very popular Ukrainian dish. It is a mildly tart vegetable soup with beets. It should retain its deep red color.

10 cups broth
2 pounds shredded cabbage
2 beets, grated
2 onions, grated
6 tomatoes, diced
½ tablespoon salt
⅛ teaspoon pepper
2 tablespoons lemon juice
2 tablespoons sugar

Use homemade, canned, or instant broth. Add all the ingredients to the broth except for the lemon juice and sugar. Cook until soft, about 25 minutes. Add the lemon juice and sugar. Heat 5 minutes longer. Serve hot.

Potato Soup

½ pound bacon
2 chopped onions
1 diced carrot
2 stalks celery, diced
4 potatoes, peeled and cubed
6 cups water
Salt and pepper to taste
Dill (optional)

Fry the bacon until it is slightly brown, but not crisp. Add the onion, celery, and carrot. Cook until the onion is translucent. Stir in the flour. Gradually add the water, stirring constantly to prevent lumps. Add potatoes and seasonings. Cook until the potatoes are tender. Garnish with the dill.

Note: Milk can be substituted for all or part of the water to make a creamier soup.

Kapusta
(Baked Sauerkraut)

1	can (16 oz.) sauerkraut
1	small head cabbage, shredded (approximately 3-4 cups)
1	onion, chopped
½	pound chopped, crisp bacon

Dash of pepper

Rinse and drain the sauerkraut. Mix all the ingredients. Bake in an ungreased casserole at 350° for one hour.

Note: *Kowbasa* or other sausage can be substituted for the bacon.

Beans and Mushrooms

2	tablespoons flour
2	tablespoons oil
1	onion, finely chopped (about 1 cup)
1	clove garlic, minced

1½ cups water

2	cans (4 oz.) mushroom slices, drained
1	can (15-16 oz.) white beans, drained

Salt and pepper to taste

Brown the flour, stirring constantly to avoid scorching. When the flour is tan, add the oil. Stir over low heat until smooth. Add the onion and garlic. Cook for several minutes. Slowly add water, stirring constantly to avoid lumps. Add the drained mushrooms and beans. Stir gently. Simmer for a few minutes until thoroughly warm. Serve hot.

Pyrohy
(Pastry-covered filling)

This recipe makes about 15-20 pyrohy, a good number for a family dinner.

1¾ cups flour
1   egg, well beaten
½   cup water
⅛   teaspoon salt
Filling

Mix all ingredients until a ball of dough forms. Knead on a lightly floured surface until smooth. Divide the dough into 2 or 3 balls. Roll one ball out until it is very thin. Cut into 3" circles. Fill with 1 tablespoon filling. Fold over and pinch the edges together or seal with the tines of a fork.

To make boiled pyrohy:

Place the *pyrohy* in a large kettle of boiling, salted water. Do not crowd, but stir occasionally to prevent sticking. Continue boiling 4 to 5 minutes after *pyrohy* start floating. Remove to a colander, rinse briefly with cold water, and toss gently with melted butter.

To make baked pyrohy:

Place the *pyrohy* on a baking sheet that has been sprayed with a cooking spray. Brush with melted butter. Bake at 375° until brown, about 7-10 minutes.

Fillings:

Savory mushroom filling:
1   tablespoon butter
1   cup onion, finely chopped.
½   pound mushrooms, finely chopped
1   slightly beaten egg
1   tablespoon chopped dill
Salt and pepper to taste

Sauté the onion in the butter. Add the mushrooms. Stir occasionally to prevent sticking and over-browning. Add the seasonings. Stir in the egg. Put about 1 tablespoon filling in each circle of dough.

Pyrohy
(Pastry-covered filling) cont.

Sweet filling:

Fig or prune filling is traditional; however, any prepared filling may be used.

Put 1 tablespoon of filling in each circle of dough.

Note: I prefer to bake the sweet *pyrohy*. When they are golden brown, brush with melted butter and sprinkle with cinnamon sugar. Serve with sour cream.

The savory *pyrohy* can be eaten as a side dish, or they can be served in soups like a filled dumpling.

Cabbage Pancakes

Much to my surprise, my family loved these! They taste much better than you might expect.

3	cups finely shredded cabbage
1	teaspoon salt
2	tablespoons butter
1	tablespoon sugar
½	cup milk
1	egg yolk
1	egg
1	cup flour

Add salt to the cabbage and let stand 30 minutes. Drain. Melt butter and add the sugar, stirring until it dissolves and begins to brown. Add cabbage and sauté until tender. Cool. Combine milk, egg, and egg yolk. Stir into flour and beat until smooth. Mix in sautéed cabbage. Pour ¼ cupfuls of batter onto hot griddle. Fry like pancakes.

Note: When you are short on time, add the sautéed cabbage to your favorite pancake mix.

Fish Balls

1   pound leftover cooked fish

¼   cup instant mashed potato flakes or ½ cup mashed potatoes

1   small onion, finely minced

2   tablespoons flour

2   tablespoons oil

½   cup broth or water

1   teaspoon salt

½   teaspoon pepper

1   teaspoon dill

1   onion, chopped

Oil or butter for frying

Mash fish into fine flakes. Mix potato, flour, finely minced onion, oil, and seasonings. Add enough liquid to moisten so the mixture will stick together. Form into balls with about one heaping tablespoon of the mixture. Carefully place the fish balls in boiling, salted water. Simmer for 10 minutes. Drain in colander.

Sauté the chopped onion in the butter or oil. Brown the fish balls in the onion and butter. Serve the fish balls with the sautéed onion.

Note: Try these with the dill sauce; recipe follows.

Dill Sauce

½   onion, finely chopped

1   tablespoon butter

2   teaspoons flour

1   cup sour cream or plain yogurt

2   teaspoons fresh dill weed

Sauté onion in the butter until transparent. Reduce heat and sprinkle the flour over onions. Blend well. Gradually stir in the sour cream. Simmer until thickened, stirring often. Stir in dill.

Note: This is a wonderful sauce to serve with fish or savory *pyrohy*. It also makes a great dip.

Cheese Pancakes

2 eggs, separated
¼ teaspoon salt
2 tablespoons sugar
2 cups cottage cheese, drained
1 cup flour
Oil for griddle

Beat egg yolks, salt, and sugar until thick. Stir in the drained cottage cheese and flour until it is smooth and well blended. Beat the egg whites in a separate bowl until they are stiff but not dry. Fold the egg whites into the cheese mixture. Drop tablespoonfuls of the pancake batter onto a hot, greased griddle. Brown the pancakes on both sides. Serve hot with sour cream.

Note: Try dusting the pancakes with a cinnamon and sugar mixture and serving with applesauce.

Dried Fruit Compote

1 pound mixed dried fruit
2 cups water
1 tablespoon honey
1 teaspoon grated lemon or orange rind
1 cinnamon stick
6 cherries, sliced

Bring fruit and water to a boil, then reduce heat. Cover and simmer until the fruit is tender. Add the rind and cinnamon stick. Sweeten with the honey. Add the cherries. Serve warm or chilled.

Note: Sprinkle with a little cinnamon before serving, if desired.

Quick Honey Cake

This is a delicious dark, heavy cake that is ideal for eating with afternoon coffee. Serve each slice with a dollop of whipped cream flavored with a dash of cinnamon for an extra rich treat.

2   eggs
1   cup sugar
1   cup honey
1   cup cooking oil
3   cups flour
1   teaspoon baking soda
2   teaspoons baking powder
1   teaspoon cinnamon
¼   teaspoon salt
1   cup milk

Beat the eggs. Continue beating while gradually adding sugar until the mixture is light and fluffy. Blend in honey, then oil, blending well after each addition. Mix dry ingredients together. Add dry ingredients alternately with milk into the honey-egg mixture. Mix until well blended. Pour into a large, greased and floured tube pan (angel food pan or bundt pan). Bake at 325° for 70 minutes.

Note: Do not peek in oven for the first 30 minutes. Be careful the oven temperature does not rise above 325° or the cake may burn.

Sift powdered sugar over the cake for decoration, if desired.

Sugar Cookies

2   cups sugar

1   cup butter or margarine

2   eggs

1   cup sour cream

1½ teaspoons baking soda

½   teaspoon salt

¾   teaspoon nutmeg

2-3 cups flour

Sugar for sprinkling (may be colored, if
    desired)

Cream the sugar and butter. Mix in the eggs and sour cream Add 2 cups of flour with the other dry ingredients. Add more flour as needed to make a dough that can be easily handled. Roll about ¼ inch thick and cut into shapes. Sprinkle with sugar.

Place cookies on a greased or sprayed baking pan. Bake at 350° for about 10 minutes or until golden.

Note: This recipe can be used to make edible Christmas tree ornaments. Roll the dough a little thicker for ornaments than you would for cookies. Use a drinking straw to cut out a hole near the top of the ornament. After the ornaments are baked and cooled, pull a thin gold ribbon or heavy thread through this hole. Enjoy your decorations on the tree until somebody eats them!

Queen Anne's Lace—Spiderweb Ornament

This makes a beautiful, delicate ornament to hang on your Christmas tree. Maybe with these webs on your tree, you will have good luck as the Czechs believe.

Fresh-cut Queen Anne's lace flowers
Large shallow box
Sand
White spray paint
Silver glitter

Gather the flowers when you find them throughout the year. Cut the stems of flowers very short. Pour a thin layer of sand in the shallow box. Carefully spread the flowers face down on the sand. Gently sift more sand over the flowers until they are completely covered. Let them dry completely, about two weeks. Lift the flowers and gently shake off the sand. Spray the dried flowers with white paint and sprinkle with the glitter.

Note: Do not wait until December to make these ornaments. Make them soon after you cut the flowers.

Co Cech to muzikant—
(Every Czech is a musician)
Czech proverb

The Czechs in Texas

Wednesday is dance night. Every week for over two decades, the Czech Folk Dancers of West, Texas, have gathered for an evening of traditional fun doing the dances their ancestors brought with them when they first came to Texas. Whole families dance, including young children who can barely walk and who occasionally fall on their bottoms with a resounding "thud." Some of these youngsters are actually grandchildren of early members of the group. They circle, twirl, clap, and shout to lively taped music and perfect their dances. Then, approximately once a month, the group performs at folk festivals throughout the state.

They would really like to perform more often, but conflicts with soccer games, occupational duties, and just modern living make it impossible. After all, the lawn still needs to be mowed, and kids still have sporting events. So the dancers do the best they can to combine life today with the treasures of the past. One such festival that celebrates the Czech culture is the Westfest held every year on Labor Day weekend. Joining the West dancers are other groups of Czech dancers from throughout the state. Each group has its own style based on the dances of the particular area or village their forebears came from.

Whenever any of these groups perform, the dancers don their gaily decorated costumes. The styles and designs of the costumes are similar to those worn by their ancestors with one major difference: The Texas costumes are made from cotton rather than the wool of Moldavia and Central Europe. With the extreme Texas heat, dancers would probably never finish a program in a wool costume! In the Parade of Costumes held at Westfest, there are many wool costumes. This is because the wearers bought the costume while visiting the regions of their ancestors' origins. The Texas-made costumes, however, are just as authentic as those from Europe because so much effort went into researching the characteristics of each area.

Beginning in the mid-1800s, thousands of Czechs left the areas of Bohemia, Moravia, Slovakia, and Silesia in Central Europe in search of a better life. At that time, these areas were under the rule of the Austrian-Hungarian empire which attempted to Germanize all its holdings. It was the strong cultural ties, rather than political ties, that bound the Czech people together. In addition, continued economic hardships and a relaxing of the laws that bound the peasants to the land made it possible for many people to consider leaving their homeland.

Inspired by glowing reports about the fertile soil and mild climate in Texas, Josef Lesikar organized a group of northern Bohemian families and obtained permission to emigrate. However, to his advantage, Lesikar's wife refused to leave her home at the last minute. The sixteen families who did leave were plagued with bad luck from the moment they set sail. Less than half of those who left Europe survived the trip to reach their new home in Austin County.

The next group of seventeen families, including Lesikar and his family, learned from the misadventures of the earlier group. They booked passage on a ship that sailed directly to Galveston in 1852, rather than making several stops en route. With them they brought supplies so they could quickly move inland, away from the diseases of the coastal lowlands that took a number from the first group. When they finally reached their destination of Cat Spring, they found an area that surpassed the glowing reports they had heard.

The early Czechs bought land for three or four dollars an acre and quickly gained a reputation for being hard workers and useful, productive citizens. Because they lived an isolated, rural life, they banded together to form fraternal organizations for the purpose of providing life insurance for the members, encouraging the study of the Czech language and culture, and providing social and cultural events. One saying goes, "Where there are two Czechs, there are three clubs" and this is not much of an exaggeration. It is largely through these organizations such as the KJT (*Katolicka Jednota Texaska* or Czech Catholic Union of Texas), KJZT (*Katolicka Podportuuijci Jednota Zen Texaskych* or Catholic Union of Czech Women of Texas), and SPJST (*Slovanska Podporujici Jednota Statu Texasu* or Slavonic Benevolent Order of the State of Texas) that the Czech heritage has been preserved. Among the first buildings in any Czech settlement was

the fraternal hall. In addition to being a communal meeting site, it also became the location of frequent Saturday night dances and various celebrations. Even today, the fraternal halls are prominent in the communities originally settled by Czechs. They are known for the dances that are often attended by just as many non-Czechs as Czechs, because they are so much fun.

Almost every family had at least one member who played a musical instrument. For dances, the accordion players and fiddlers joined together to play all the popular and traditional dance music that was passed down from one generation to the next. Among the unusual traditional instruments in Czech bands in Texas is the hammered dulcimer. This is a Moravian instrument with 120 strings that are struck with wooden mallets. Another is the *tamburash*, a lute-like Bohemian instrument invented over four hundred years ago. So important was music and being able to play an instrument, that the proverb *Co Cech to muzikant* (Every Czech is a musician) stated an understood point of pride.

To the early Czechs who lived an isolated life, weddings were a particularly festive social occasion. First, the young couple had to arrange for the rental of land to farm until they could afford to buy their own land. Friends of the groom would then visit neighboring farms to issue formal invitations to everyone in the community. A few days before the ceremony, the Czech women would gather at the bride's home to begin preparing the food for the wedding breakfast before the ceremony and the reception afterwards.

On the way to the bride's home, the church parish hall, or, more likely, the fraternal hall, for the reception, the guests were usually stopped by a ribbon stretched across the road. Friends of the bridal couple asked for gifts of money for the newlyweds in return for permission to pass. As the guests arrived at their destination, the bridesmaids pinned a sprig of rosemary, the symbol of fidelity and constancy, on each guest.

In the early days, the feast that followed often consisted of pork, goose, and chicken, as well as many different varieties of the traditional *klobase* (sausage), *kolaches*, and *strudel* and plenty of beer. A traditional band provided music for dancing. Czech weddings today are very similar. There is always lots of food, dancing, and beer. The food may be Texas barbecue or a Tex-Mex dinner, but it will always be served with beer and *kolaches*.

Christmas is more than just a day of celebration for the Czechs. It is an entire season to celebrate and to foretell the future. The pioneer families began their celebration on December 8, the Feast of the Immaculate Conception. *Matcka*, the Blessed Mother, put gifts of fruit and nuts in the shoes of good boys and girls. Even today many Czech children receive small gifts on December 8. One superstition for this day states that the weather on Christmas Day will be the same as it is on this day.

Today, as in the early days, carolers go from house to house singing *koledy* (gift songs) of hymns and carols and then are rewarded afterwards with sweets. One popular carol, "Good King Wenceslas" was written about a Bohemian prince-duke in the tenth century. In "We are Going to the Stable," each shepherd on the way to see the Christ Child plays a different instrument, and the words of the song imitate the sounds of each one. Czech choral clubs and fraternal organizations from throughout the state keep the custom of caroling alive today, even the singing of "Silent Night" in Czech, *"Ticha Noc, Svata Noc."*

For weeks before Christmas, Czech cooks are busy doing their holiday baking. They bake the traditional foods such as *kolaches*, *vanocka* (a Christmas coffee cake), or *pernik na figurky*, a type of gingerbread cookie. Christmas Eve, according to church ritual, is supposed to be a day of fasting, an almost impossible feat with all the smells of tempting dishes and treats. Children were promised that they would see the *zlate prasatko* or "golden pig" in the evening if they resisted the temptation and did not eat all day. To this day, no one has ever seen the "golden pig" because no one has been able to resist the sights and smells of the cooking foods.

Christmas Eve supper is an elaborate meal, usually featuring carp or some other fish. Before electricity, the candles on the tree were lit and the children were allowed in to see it for the first time. The wondrous sight of the lit tree was made even more glorious in their eyes because it was decorated with fruits, nuts, and homemade cookies. After all, plastic had not yet been invented, so they had to use things that they had made themselves! But after all the revelry at home, most Czechs attend midnight mass to remember the religious significance of the holiday.

The holiday lasts until St. Stephen's Day on December 26, when people are able to relax with relatives and other family members and eat Christmas leftovers. After all the cooking and baking to get ready for Christmas, the women definitely need the day off to recover!

On St. Stephen's Day, the Czech people played many different games designed to foretell the future. Superstitions abounded at this time. Once taken seriously, they are now part of the fun and lore of the season. For example, it was believed that if a gun were shot off on Christmas Eve, evil spirits would be driven away. Today, fireworks and sparklers, rather than gunpowder, are more likely to be used. And, of course, everyone enjoys the beauty of the colorful display in the skies. Another form of fortune-telling was the reading of tarot cards.

On New Year's Eve, the Czechs celebrate with the same enthusiasm as

they do everything else. Their favorite form of revelry is, of course, dancing! Regardless of what kind of band provides the music—be it a professional group or a neighborhood scratch band—there will always be polkas and rollicking Czech dances in Texas. Dancing, whether it is a traditional folk dance, the polka, or the Texas two-step, is one important facet of early Czech life that is still paramount today.

After World War I, Czechoslovakia was reunited into a separate, independent country. Today, more than twenty communities throughout Texas have annual Czech festivals featuring singing, dancing, and traditional foods. Although the Czechs originally settled in Austin, Fayette, Lavaca, and Washington Counties, they did branch out to other areas throughout the state. Today Czech is the fourth most frequently spoken language in Texas.

Czech Recipes

Koprova Omacka
(Dill Soup)

2½ cups water

3 medium potatoes, peeled and cubed

1 teaspoon salt

1 tablespoon flour

1 cup half and half or milk

2 tablespoons fresh dill, finely chopped

3 hard-boiled eggs, chopped

Boil the potatoes in salted water. When the potatoes are almost cooked, add flour and half and half. Bring the soup to a full boil. Add the dill. Garnish with the chopped eggs.

Note: Try adding a little vinegar to this soup.

For a smooth soup, put it in the blender or food processor before adding the flour and cream.

Sauerkraut Relish

1   can (14 oz.) sauerkraut
1   cup chopped celery
½   cup chopped carrots
½   cup chopped onion
½   cup chopped green pepper
¾   cup sugar
½   cup vinegar
⅓   cup salad oil

Chop the vegetables in a food processor. Drain and rinse the sauerkraut, then mix with chopped vegetables. Mix sugar, vinegar, and oil together. Pour over the kraut mixture. Cover tightly and refrigerate at least several hours before serving.

Note: This keeps for a long time in the refrigerator.

Creamed Cabbage

1   small head cabbage

Take off the outside leaves of the cabbage, cut into quarters, and remove the center core from each quarter. Soak in cold, salted water for 20 minutes. Cook in a small amount of boiling water for 15-30 minutes. Do not overcook.

Cream Sauce:
2   tablespoons butter or margarine
2   tablespoons flour
Dash of pepper
¼   teaspoon salt
1   cup cream or milk
½   cup grated cheese (optional)
Cracker crumbs

Melt butter in a small pan. Add flour mixed with seasonings and stir until well blended. (A wire whisk will make it easy to keep sauce smooth and free of lumps.) Pour cream in gradually, stirring constantly. Bring to a boil. Boil 2 minutes, stirring constantly. Add grated cheese, if desired.

Layer cabbage and sauce in a greased or sprayed casserole dish. Sprinkle the top layer with cracker crumbs. Bake at 325° for 20-30 minutes.

Note: To save calories and fat, I have even used skim milk when making the sauce. It is not quite as rich as when I use cream, but it is still very good!

Wedding Noodles

2 egg yolks
2 cups flour
Pinch of salt
Broth or soup

Mix the egg yolks, flour, and salt to make moderately stiff dough. Knead until smooth. Roll the dough as thinly as possible into a rectangle. Place a towel over a chair back. Drape the dough over the towel and let dry for about 1½ hours.

Do not allow to dry until stiff! Roll the dough tightly like you would for a jellyroll. Slice the dough as narrowly as possible. Add the noodles to your favorite broth or soup and boil for 15 minutes.

Note: According to Czech tradition, the thinner the noodles, the better the noodles!

Tomato Gravy

3 tablespoons cooking oil
¼ cup chopped onion
2 tablespoons flour
1 can (15 oz.) chopped tomatoes
2 tablespoons sugar
Cream or milk
Salt
Pepper

Sauté the onion in the oil. Add the flour and brown. Pour in the liquid from the tomatoes and stir until smooth. Add the tomatoes and sugar, stirring constantly. Add the cream to make the gravy the desired consistency. Season with salt and pepper to taste.

Czech Goulash

The cabbage in this easy recipe gives the stew a different but great flavor.

1½ pounds stew meat

1   large onion, diced

1   can (8 oz.) tomato sauce

1   clove garlic

2   stalks celery, diced

3   medium potatoes, diced

3   medium carrots, diced

1½ cups cabbage, shredded

1   teaspoon salt

1   teaspoon pepper

1   heaping tablespoon flour

Cut meat into bite-size cubes and rinse in cold water. Place meat in a large pot and cover with water, approximately 3 cups. Bring to a boil and skim foam as it appears. Add celery, onion, garlic, salt, pepper, and tomato sauce to meat. Cover and simmer for 1 to 1½ hours.

Dice the vegetables in a food processor. Cook the potatoes and carrots, but reserve the liquid. Cook the cabbage and drain. Add potatoes, carrots, and cabbage to the meat mixture. Mix flour with the reserved liquid from the potatoes. Stir into the meat mixture for thickening. Boil slowly for an additional 30 minutes, stirring occasionally.

Note: Add your favorite seasonings to give this recipe your own signature. Allspice is good if you want to keep the Czech flavor. For a Texas version, add bottled barbecue sauce, liquid smoke, or picante sauce. Use your imagination!

Cabbage-Sausage Casserole

1   small head cabbage
1   pound pork sausage
⅓   cup uncooked rice
½   cup chopped onion
1   can (8 oz.) tomato sauce
⅔   cup water

Brown crumbled sausage and onion. Drain. Spray a deep casserole dish with a cooking spray. Spread rice on the bottom of the dish. Cut the cabbage into medium-size pieces and place on top of rice. Top with the sausage-onion mixture. Pour the tomato sauce and water over the top. Bake at 350° for about 1 hour until the cabbage is tender.

Note: Serve with either corn bread or a hearty dark bread for a great supper!

Bozí Milosti
(God's Favors)

Once you taste these, you will agree with the name!

3   eggs
1   tablespoon butter or margerine
2¾ cups flour
3   tablespoons sugar
3   tablespoons milk
Oil for frying
Sifted powdered sugar or cinnamon sugar
    for dusting

Mix together the eggs, sugar, butter, and milk. Add the flour and then mix well. The dough will be similar to pie dough. Roll out as thinly as possible. Cut into strips or squares. Fry in the oil until golden brown. Drain on paper towels. Dust with powdered sugar or cinnamon sugar.

Czech Apple Strudel

The secret is out! Anyone can make delicious apple strudel! You will be surprised at how easy this is to make.

Dough:
- ½ cup milk
- 1 tablespoon butter or margarine
- 1 egg yolk
- 1 tablespoon sugar
- 1½ cups flour

Filling:
- 1 can (15 oz.) sliced apples
- ½ cup sugar
- ½ cup brown sugar
- 1 teaspoon cinnamon
- ½ cup melted butter or margarine

Any or all of the following optional ingredients:
- ½ cup chopped maraschino cherries
- ½ cup chopped nuts
- ½ cup coconut
- ½ cup raisins

Scald butter and milk; let it cool. Beat egg yolk and sugar together. Add cooled liquid. Gradually stir in flour. Mix well. Knead on floured surface until the dough forms a smooth ball. Cover the dough until it is warm and pliable—about 25-35 minutes. Dust flour on a large pastry cloth. (If you do not have a pastry cloth, a clean linen or cotton cup towel will do. Do not use a terry towel.) Roll and stretch the dough as thin as possible on the pastry cloth. Do not allow the dough to tear!

Mix the sugars and cinnamon together. Spread the apples over the dough, leaving about an inch at the bottom of the dough. Evenly sprinkle the optional items over the apples. Sprinkle the sugar mixture over the filling. Drizzle about ⅔ of the melted butter over the sugar. Lift the pastry cloth, peeling it back as you roll up the strudel. Pinch the ends of the dough together to seal. Brush with the rest of the melted butter. Bake at 350° for 35-45 minutes until golden. Decorate with powdered sugar icing, if desired.

Note: If the canned apples are sliced too thickly, chop or slice them so the strudel will roll more easily.

If you are short on time, use canned apple pie filling. Omit the sugars and cinnamon, but add any of the optional ingredients you want to make the strudel uniquely yours!

Kolaches

We all think of kolaches first when we think of Czech food!

1　package rapid rise yeast
¼　cup water
¾　cup milk
½　cup butter or margarine
¼　cup sugar
1　teaspoon salt
3¾-4½ cups flour
2　eggs
Filling
Streusel topping

Scald the milk. Add the butter and water. Remove from heat once the butter has melted and cool slightly. Mix the sugar, salt, yeast, and 3 cups of flour together. Add the warm milk mixture to the flour and mix well. Mix in the eggs. Add as much additional flour as needed to make a firm, easily handled dough. Knead until smooth on a floured surface. Roll into a ball in a greased bowl. Cover and let rest for 10 minutes. Shape into balls and place in greased pans. Cover and place in a warm, draft-free place until double in size.

Make an indentation in the center of each ball. Fill with a filling. Sprinkle the streusel topping over the filling. Bake at 375° for 15-20 minutes or until golden.

Lemon-Cheese Filling:
1　carton (16 oz.) large-curd cottage cheese
1　box (3¾ oz.) instant lemon pudding

Combine in a blender or food processor until smooth.

Streusel Topping:
¾　cup sugar
1　cup flour
½　cup melted butter.
¼　cup cinnamon, if desired

Mix all ingredients until crumbly. Sprinkle over the kolache filling before baking.

Note: Prepared fruit filling or pie filling can be used for fruit kolaches.

Vanocka
(Christmas Braid)

In many families, the mother or grandmother made this sweet bread as a special treat for her family on Christmas Eve. Any leftovers were toasted with butter for breakfast on Christmas morning.

1　package rapid rise yeast
¼　cup warm water
2　cups scalded milk
⅓　cup butter or margarine
½　cup sugar
1　teaspoon salt
1　slightly beaten egg
5-7　cups flour
1　cup chopped almonds
½　cup mixed candied fruit
½　cup white raisins
1　egg, beaten with 1 tablespoon water

Scald the milk and add butter and water. Remove from heat once the butter has melted. Cool slightly. Mix yeast, sugar, and 1½ cups flour in a large bowl. Add warm, not hot, liquids. Beat until smooth. Cover and let rest for about 10 minutes. Add ½ cup almonds, fruit, and raisins. Mix in enough flour to make a soft dough—about 4-5 cups. Knead dough until elastic. Cover and let rest about 10 minutes. Divide into 5 parts. Roll 3 of the parts into long, thick "snakes." Make a braid with these 3 "snakes." Brush with the egg mixed with water. Twist together the 2 remaining parts. Place on top of the larger braid. Brush with the beaten egg. Sprinkle with the remaining ½ cup chopped almonds. Cover and let rise in warm spot until about double—about 45 minutes. Bake at 350° for 45 minutes.

Note: This is so good just plain that there is no need to decorate *vanocka* with powdered sugar icing, unless you want to "gild the lily"!

Czech Nog with Rum

Be careful! This tastes so good, you may be tempted to keep drinking!

5   tablespoons powdered sugar
1   can (15 oz.) condensed milk
1   teaspoon vanilla
1½ cups rum
⅔   cup scalded milk, cooled

Combine the sugar, condensed milk, and vanilla. Mix in the rum. Add the cool, scalded milk. Mix thoroughly. Pour into a container with a lid. Keep in the refrigerator until cold and ready to serve.

Note: Omit the rum and add ½ teaspoon rum flavoring for a nonalcoholic version of this holiday nog.

Mazel Tov, Ya'll—
Jews in Texas

Eight second-graders sat in a circle on the floor of their Sunday school classroom clutching a favorite stuffed animal or doll that was about to receive a name. The group discussed each name and what it meant before participating in the Jewish naming ceremony. Little giggles punctuated the seriousness of the occasion as prayers were said for the Beanie Babies and teddy bears. By the time each toy had been named, the children knew the meaning behind the ceremony and appreciated another aspect of their heritage. Many of the ancient traditions and rituals are still practiced in Texas by the Jews.

Although Jews came to Texas with the conquistadors and have been scattered about the state since before it was a republic, it was not until the 1870s that the first concentrated wave of immigration began. With the completion of the railroad, some Jews who had immigrated through New York then came to Texas. Many were originally merchants and entrepreneurs from Germany who had heard of the opportunities in this exotic land far away.

A second wave from Eastern Europe occurred about a decade later. This group of immigrants had faced religious persecution and had escaped to find a place where they could practice the Orthodox form of their religion.

When they arrived in Texas, the Jews already here seemed almost like a different breed entirely. To the newcomers, they seemed almost more Texan than Jewish because they had adapted their everyday lives to the economic realities of their new home.

The largest wave of immigration began in 1907 with the Galveston Movement. Ultimately, 10,000 Jews would enter Texas through this program. Immigrants were encouraged to go to Galveston rather than New York where anti-immigration sentiments were unfolding. In addition, the Jewish population in New York was increasing faster than jobs could be found for the newcomers. Galveston was chosen over other ports because it connected with a German passenger shipping line that could bring the immigrants directly to

Texas. Also, railroad lines radiated from Galveston Island so immigrants could quickly proceed to the rest of the state as well as to the Midwest and other sections of the United States. Though Galveston was the fourth largest city in Texas at this time, it was still small enough to encourage the immigrants to leave the area quickly in order to find jobs. Galveston was not large enough to even attempt to provide jobs for everyone coming in.

Although large numbers of Eastern European Jews desperately wanted to come to the United States where they would be free from religious persecution, Texas was not the first choice for many. Unlike other immigrants who heard stories of cheap land and riches to be had in Texas, the Jews heard tales of discrimination. Jobs required work on Saturday, their traditional Sabbath. Plus, Texas lacked kosher butchers.

Rabbi Henry Cohen greeted those who did arrive in Galveston after three long weeks at sea. Rabbi Cohen had come to Galveston in 1888 to serve the almost one thousand Jews on the island. He quickly became a noted community leader and activist. After the hurricane that devastated the island on September 8, 1900, Rabbi Cohen worked with Clara Barton, the organizer of the American Red Cross, in relief efforts to help the entire city, not just the Jews. On Sunday morning after the storm, Cohen opened the doors of B'nai Israel, the Jewish temple, to Christians whose churches were demolished. He appointed himself prime advocate for the Jews who arrived in Galveston. He made sure they were fed and clothed and then helped them find the public baths and ultimately jobs. Frequently he made small loans to the newcomers right on the wharf so they could start new businesses at their destinations.

When the first group succeeded, they brought over their relatives to join them. The result was a number of scattered enclaves of Jews in small towns throughout the state. Most eventually realized the American dream of prosperity by becoming successful merchants and businessmen, often with the help of the loans given them on the Galveston wharfs by Rabbi Cohen. A number were sent to Tyler, Texarkana, Marshall, and Palestine because the train fare to these areas was low. It was this project that brought Jews to El Campo, Bay City, Edna, and Wharton in Wharton County, south of Houston. The descendants of the original immigrants still drive thirty or more miles to attend services on Friday nights. This is the same situation in other small towns across the state.

The immigrant Jews brought with them a centuries-old set of religious practices that affected all aspects of everyday life. Included were the dietary laws dictating that animals were to be slaughtered in a certain way by a *shochet,* meat and dairy products were never to be eaten together, and certain

foods (i.e., shellfish, pork, etc.) were not to be eaten at all. Within the laws of *Kashrut* (kosher), Jews have always adapted their eating to their surroundings. Jews, like non-Jews, always ate whatever was available. People from Eastern Europe ate more lamb than those from Northern Europe, who ate more cabbage and potatoes because these were the foods most readily accessible to them. The Jews slaughtered animals in a different manner than other people and ate different combinations of foods. Like everyone else, however, they could only eat from the choices available.

This is exactly what happened when the Jews came to Texas. The Orthodox immigrants who came during the Galveston Movement immediately realized that a lack of kosher butchers was indeed a fact and not just a rumor. Sometimes a rabbi, where there was a rabbi, was assigned this job. He was also given the job of *mohel* (the one who circumcises male babies), unlike in Europe and the East Coast where specialists performed these duties. However, many Jews found themselves scattered throughout the state in small towns that were unable to support or entice a rabbi to come on any regular basis to perform these duties. The practicality of life in Texas dictated that some of the strict Jewish laws could not be kept. So, although the meat may not have been kosher, it was still prepared in the same way as before. *Challah*, a braided bread made especially for the Sabbath and

holidays, was and still is an important part of the Friday night meal.

In rabbinate circles, Texas was considered a theological and intellectual wasteland. Relocating to the western wilderness was akin to exile. The few rabbis who did come to Texas during these early days found distinct conflicts between two groups of Jews. One group consisted of the recent arrivals from Europe, who followed the Orthodox ways and who spoke their native language and Yiddish (an Eastern European language that combines Hebrew and German) but not English. The other group was comprised of those who had come to Texas after living in other parts of the United States. Some were even first-generation Americans. This group, for the most part, had accepted the fact that they could not close their stores on Saturday for the Sabbath because that was the biggest shopping day of the week.

Many Jews adjusted to eating non-kosher meat, though many maintained the ban against pork and shellfish. Others continued to strictly observe the Orthodox Jewish laws. And still others chose to follow the more liberal Reform movement. The different levels of adherence to the dietary rules is only one of the differences among the Orthodox, Conservative, and Reform forms of Judaism. In areas where the Jewish population was not large enough to support more than one synagogue, the rabbi had to negotiate a compromise between the different members.

The Jewish Sabbath (*Shabbot*) begins at sundown on Friday and continues until sundown on Saturday. Traditionally, this was a time for worship, study, and rest, and not a time for work. Very quickly the new immigrants learned that working on Saturday rather than attending services was an economic necessity. Rabbis adapted by preaching their strongest message on Friday night rather than Saturday morning when attendance would be very light. In later years when Friday night became the official time for high school football, the weekly game usually drew more attendance than the services. To avoid conflicts with the secular world, some synagogues have started beginning their Saturday services early in the morning so worshippers can be finished in time to begin their day's work. Also, to be consistent with the religious practices of other groups in Texas, religious education is often given to the children in Sunday schools, just like in the churches.

Even animals were given a day of rest on *Shabbat*, which meant that one was not to ride a horse or ride in a carriage and later, by extension, drive a car. This worked fine in Germany or Prussia where Jews lived in confined ghettos or in the major cities such as Houston or Dallas where large numbers of Jews lived in proximity of each other and a temple. It did/does not work in rural Texas where the distances are so much greater. To

attend services at all, Jews often had to travel ten, twenty, or even more miles. And this meant driving. Today there are still some areas where it is possible to maintain the Orthodox standards, but these are mainly in the larger cities where Jews can live close enough to walk to services and there is a large enough population to support the dietary laws.

The ban against working on the *Shabbat* extended to include a ban against cooking. But people still had to eat. Before sundown on Friday night the women would put on a large pot of a stew that is sometimes described as a type of Jewish chili. It simmers until the next day. Unlike other religions where the women worked their hardest to prepare the Sabbath meal, the Jewish women actually got the day off!

According to Jewish law, the purposes of marriage are the maintenance of family life, procreation, and companionship. With the emphasis on families, the young couple is escorted to the *chappah* (wedding canopy where the ceremony is performed) by both sets of parents. The *chappah* symbolizes the new home the couple is forming. During the ceremony the rabbi recites the betrothal benediction over a glass of wine. Then the bride and groom sip from the glass. After the vows are said, the marriage contract is read, and the seven blessings are read, the groom smashes the wineglass with his foot.

This symbolizes the destruction of the temple in Jerusalem centuries ago. Then the celebration begins! Everyone wishes the couple *mazel tov* (good luck) and enjoys much too much good food.

Passover is a time when food plays a significant role in Jewish traditions. To commemorate the haste with which the Jews left Egypt, they do not eat anything with yeast or leavening. The traditional food to eat is *matzos*, similar to large, unsalted crackers. This is also a time when no lamb is eaten because lamb's blood was put on the doorposts so the Angel of Death could pass over the Jewish households in Egypt. At the traditional Passover *Seder* a roasted bone is on the platter to represent the lamb. Also on the *Seder* plate are bitter herbs, an egg, a green vegetable, saltwater, and a fruit. Each food has a special meaning and is part of the Passover service. Even today, extended families gather in someone's home for the Passover *Seder*.

Shavorut comes seven weeks after Passover. It commemorates the giving of the *Torah* on Mt. Sinai. This was also when the Jews received the dietary laws of *Kashrut*.

One aspect of Jewish life that is still of prime importance is the celebration of the high holy days and Jewish New Year. These are the celebrations of *Yom Kippur* and *Rosh Hashanah*. On these days, stores owned by Jews will be closed, children will miss school, and everyone will be worshipping in the synagogue. Men will wear a *yarmulke* (skullcap) as they do whenever they enter a synagogue as well as a *tallis* (prayer shawl), which is generally worn only for special occasions. On *Yom Kippur*, many will fast, as is dictated by Jewish law. To make it possible to go twenty-four hours without eating, the last meal before the fast is large and very filling. On the evening of *Yom Kippur*, the fast is broken with a buffet of traditional foods. These will generally include chopped liver, gefilte fish, bagels and whole grain breads, and eggs.

Hanukah is a more social than religious time. It is called the Festival of Lights because it celebrates the miracle of the oil, where a small amount of oil lasted for eight days and nights. To commemorate the oil, fried foods, especially latkes (potato pancakes), are traditional. The giving of gifts after the lighting of the candles in the menorah on each of the eight days is relatively recent. Some claim this to be the Jewish answer to Santa Claus, but of course it is even better because the gift-giving lasts for eight days rather than one! Some Jewish families do celebrate a secular "Christmas" which includes Santa and gifts but no religious message.

Today it is much easier to be kosher than it was in the past. Kosher meats are available in larger cities, and transportation makes it possible for people in smaller towns to have kosher products on a regular basis. However, this is

Texas, and Jews have always adapted to their surroundings while maintaining their own traditions. That is why today you will see such events as kosher chili cook-offs!

Though there may be beans in the chili—an addition often debated by Texans—there will not be cheese!

Jewish Recipes

Birkat Adonai hi ta-ashir
The blessing of the Lord, it maketh rich.
Proverbs 10:22

Kugel
(Noodle Pudding)

1	package (8 oz.) thin noodles
4	eggs
1	stick butter or margarine, melted
½	cup grated cheese
1	cup cold milk

Cook the noodles; drain. Combine the eggs, butter, and noodles in a buttered casserole. Pour milk over the top. Top with the cheese. Bake at 300° for about an hour until a knife inserted in the center comes out clean.

Blintzes

Filling:

16   ounces dry cottage cheese
1   package (8 oz.) cream cheese
3   teaspoons sugar
1   egg
¼   teaspoon cinnamon
½   teaspoon salt

Completely mix together.

Batter:

3   eggs
2   tablespoons melted butter
½   cup flour
½   cup milk

Beat together the eggs. Slowly add flour, then milk. Add the melted butter to a small skillet and heat. Add enough batter to make a very thin pancake—about a tablespoon. Tip the pan from side to side to cover the bottom of the pan. Cook on one side until it bubbles. Remove to toweling. Repeat until all the batter has been used. Put a rounded tablespoon of cheese mixture in the center of each pancake Fold over from both sides, then the ends into an envelope.

Just before serving, fry on both sides in butter, or dot with butter and bake at 350° degrees until golden brown—about 20 minutes. Serve hot. Garnish with sour cream or preserves, if desired.

Borscht
(Beet Soup)

This is a beautiful pink soup that is extremely easy to make.

1   can (15 oz.) beets
1½   cups sour cream
Juice of 1 lemon
Salt and pepper to taste

Drain the beets, but reserve the liquid. Mix the liquid with the sour cream until the color is uniform. Process the beets and lemon juice in a blender or food processor until smooth. Mix the beets and sour cream until the color is uniform. Salt and pepper to taste. Serve with a dollop of sour cream in each bowl. Garnish with fresh dill.

Potato Latkes

These are a favorite throughout the year, but especially during Hanukah when fried foods are important.

4   potatoes, peeled, grated, and drained
1   onion, grated
1   egg
3   tablespoons flour
¼   teaspoon black pepper
½   teaspoon baking powder
1   teaspoon salt
½   cup shortening or oil

Mix together everything except the oil. Heat the shortening or oil in a skillet or on a griddle. Drop by ¼ cupfuls onto the hot skillet. Brown the latkes on both sides. Drain well. Serve with applesauce or catsup.

Note: Use your food processor to grate the potatoes and onion. A cooking spray can be used in place of most of the shortening or oil. Try adding a half-teaspoon of garlic powder!

Coleslaw Vinaigrette

1   small head cabbage
1   green pepper
2   carrots

Vinaigrette:

½   teaspoon salt
½   teaspoon dry mustard
¾   teaspoon celery salt
2   tablespoons sugar
1   tablespoon chopped pimiento
2   teaspoons grated onion
3   tablespoons salad oil
⅓   cup white vinegar

Shred the vegetables in a food processor. Mix the vegetables in a bowl.

Whisk the vinaigrette ingredients together. Pour over the vegetables and mix thoroughly. Refrigerate overnight, if possible, but at least for several hours so the flavors can blend. Serve at room temperature.

Note: Garnish with green pepper rings, thin tomato wedges, sprigs of celery tops or chopped cilantro, if desired.

Peach Kugel

Children love to eat the leftovers cold!

1 package (8 oz.) wide egg noodles
3 tablespoons butter or margarine
3 eggs
½ cup sugar
¼ teaspoon salt
2 cups milk
1 can (16 oz.) sliced peaches, drained

Streusel Topping:

6 crushed crackers
½ teaspoon cinnamon

Cook the noodles; drain. Stir in the butter. In a separate bowl blend the eggs, sugar, and salt. Stir in milk. Stir milk and egg mixture into the noodles. Pour into a greased 1½-quart glass baking dish. Bake 30 minutes at 350°. Arrange peach slices over the top. Mix cracker crumbs and cinnamon and sprinkle over the top. Return to the oven for an additional 15 minutes. For easier cutting, let stand 30 minutes before serving.

Note: Buttery crackers such as Ritz or Waverly Wafers are especially good in the streusel topping, but matzos will work also.

Half a cup of seedless raisins may be added to the milk and egg mixture, if desired.

Chopped Liver

1 pound chicken liver
5 hard-boiled eggs
1 onion

Cook the livers and let cool. In small batches, process liver, eggs, and onion in a food processor until it is very fine. Season to taste.

Note: For variety, add any or all of the following before processing: 1 teaspoon Worcestershire, extra hard-boiled eggs, and 2 tablespoons chicken fat. After mixing, add 1 cup chopped celery or shredded carrots for color and crunch.

Sweet and Sour Pot Roast

1   rump roast
2   large onions, cut
2   bay leaves
2   tablespoons lemon juice
3   tablespoons catsup
1   tablespoon brown sugar
½   cup raisins
Salt and pepper to taste

Season the roast with salt and pepper. Brown the roast on all sides in a Dutch oven. Pour off all the fat. Add the onions and bay leaves. Cover and simmer for 1 hour. Add the lemon juice, catsup, brown sugar, and raisins. Continue simmering until tender.

To make gravy (optional):

Remove everything except the liquid from the pan. Crush 4-5 gingersnaps into ½ cup water. Add the cookies and water. Stir until the gravy is smooth and thickened.

Note: The gingersnaps give the gravy some real pizzazz!

Honey Orange Chicken

This is a favorite dish for Rosh Hashanah, the Jewish New Year. However, it is so delicious and easy, it is good any time of the year!

1	chicken, cut into serving pieces or about 3-4 pounds chicken pieces
½	cup bread crumbs
½	teaspoon salt
⅛	teaspoon pepper
1	egg
1	teaspoon water
¼	cup vegetable oil
½	cup hot water
⅛	cup honey
½	cup orange juice
1	tablespoon freshly grated ginger

Beat the egg and water in one bowl. In another bowl, mix the bread crumbs, salt, and pepper. Dip the chicken pieces into the egg mixture and then in the bread crumbs. Brown in the oil. Mix together the hot water, honey, and orange juice. Put the chicken in an ovenproof dish with a cover. Pour the honey mixture over the chicken. Sprinkle with the ginger. Cover and bake at 325° for 45 minutes.

Note: ½ teaspoon ground ginger can be substituted for the fresh ginger.

Chicken Soup

No collection of Jewish recipes would be complete without chicken soup. Medical science has proven what Jews have known for centuries—this soup works miracles to relieve congestion.

3-4   pounds chicken
3-4   quarts water
1   onion, sliced
2   stalks celery, sliced
1   tablespoon salt
¼   teaspoon pepper

Rinse the chicken under cool, running water. Put all the ingredients in a large pot. Cover tightly and simmer for 3 or more hours until the chicken is tender. Cool and remove the chicken to be used in another recipe. Remove the fat that has congealed on top. Strain the broth (optional). Season to taste. Cook noodles, matzo balls, or whatever you like in the hot soup. Serve hot and enjoy!

Note: Unless you are serving this to guests or are very particular about your soup, you can forego straining the soup. Debone a cup or two of chicken to add to the stock, add about the same amount of frozen mixed vegetables and then some noodles, matzo balls, rice, etc. This makes a wonderful, nourishing meal for both the patient and the healthy!

Kneydlakh
(Matzo Balls)

3   eggs

1   teaspoon salt

1   cup matzo meal

3   tablespoons chicken fat

OR

3   tablespoons butter or margarine plus 3 tablespoons chicken broth

Mix all the ingredients together. Refrigerate for at least an hour until all the liquid is absorbed. Shape into balls 1 inch in diameter. Drop into a large pot of boiling salted water. Reduce heat to medium, cover, and cook for 30 minutes. Remove with a slotted spoon and place in a soup bowl. Pour hot soup into the bowl.

Note: There are many variations to this recipe. Some cooks add dried, minced onion or chopped parsley. Others insist that the eggs be separated or that the pot not be covered. Experiment and decide for yourself how you like your matzo balls!

Leftovers can be browned in butter the next day and then sprinkled with cinnamon and sugar for a filling treat.

Challah
(Rich Egg Bread)

Challah is an important part of the Friday night meal. In the past, Jewish women would make the bread for the entire week on Friday so the Shabbat challah would be fresh. This recipe is simpler than most and only makes one loaf.

1   package rapid rise yeast
¼   cup water
½   cup milk
1   tablespoon sugar
1   teaspoon salt
1   egg
1   tablespoon shortening
2¾-3½ cups flour

Glaze:
1   egg yolk
2   tablespoons cold water

Mix 2 cups flour, yeast, salt, and sugar. Heat the shortening, water, and milk until very warm. Stir the liquids into the dry ingredients. Add the egg. Mix in as much flour as is needed to make a firm dough. Knead until smooth. Cover dough and let it rest for 10 minutes. Divide the dough into three sections. Roll each section into a strand 14 inches long. Braid the three strands. Pinch the ends together and tuck them under the loaf securely. Cover and let rise in a warm, draft-free place until doubled in size. Mix the egg yolk and cold water together and brush on the braid. Bake at 375° for 25-30 minutes.

Note: Sprinkle sesame or poppy seeds over the glaze, if desired.

Mandel Bread

4   eggs
1½ cups sugar
4   tablespoons evaporated milk
1   stick butter or margarine
1   cup shortening
1   teaspoon salt
1   cup chopped pecans
1   teaspoon vanilla
1   teaspoon almond flavoring
6   cups flour

Cream together the eggs, sugar, and milk. Add shortening and butter. Add remaining ingredients. Shape into loaves on a cookie sheet. The loaves should be about 1 inch high and 3 inches wide. Bake 10 minutes at 400°, then 20 minutes at 300°. Remove from the oven and slice about ½ inch thick. Arrange slices on a cookie sheet. Dry in the oven at 150° until as dry and crisp as you like it, probably at least 30 minutes.

Note: This is similar to biscotti, which is so popular in coffee shops. Dip one end in either white or dark chocolate for an extra-special treat.

Chopped almonds or other nuts can also be used.

This is actually a very simple recipe that gives delicious results!

Sponge Cake

This is a feather-light dessert. Serve it with fruit or just plain.

6 eggs, separated
Grated rind of 1 orange
1 cup sugar
1½ cups flour
1½ teaspoons baking powder
¼ teaspoon salt
½ cup orange juice
½ teaspoon cream of tartar

Grease the tube of a 10-inch tube pan. Line the bottom of the pan with waxed paper. Beat the egg yolks well. Add the orange rind and sugar. Beat until the mixture is light and thickened. Add the flour alternately with the orange juice, beginning and ending with the flour. Whip the egg whites with the baking powder, cream of tartar, and salt until stiff peaks form. Gently fold the whites into the batter. Bake at 325° for 1 hour. Invert the cake pan until the cake is completely cool—at least several hours. Remove the cake from the pan and serve as soon as possible.

A People Without a Country—

The Wends in Texas

Monday is noodle-making day in Serbin, Texas. Every Monday descendants of the original Slavic settlers from Lusatia, a region of what is now Germany, gather at the Texas Wendish Heritage Museum to laugh, gossip, and make over one hundred thirty pounds of authentic Wendish noodles.

The recipe calls for five twenty-five-pound bags of flour, thirty-three dozen eggs, and salt. All morning the ladies pour the ingredients into the noodle machine and hand cut fresh strips of pasta as they spew onto the screen mesh drying frames. By the middle of the afternoon, every counter and tabletop is covered with screens of drying noodles. Since the 1980s Wendish volunteers have been making these noodles to sell at the museum gift shop, local stores, and ethnic festivals throughout the area. But Wendish women

have been making noodles in Texas ever since they first arrived in this country in the mid-eighteen hundreds.

The noodle-makers are descendants of the six hundred immigrants who left their native land in 1854, not only in search of prosperity, but also in search of religious liberty and the right to speak their Wendish language. Only a small area along the River Spree in the old country was inhabited by true Wends, an ancient Slavic people who claim to be descendants of Japheth, son of Noah. Prussian insistence that the Wends speak and use the German language, economic reform laws that discriminated against the Wends, and the government's insistence they join the state church caused many to make the decision to leave their home country. One group settled in Australia and the other group came to Texas. Outside of Germany, these are the only two areas where Wends have settled.

Reverend Jan Kilian organized the brave pioneers who sailed on the three-masted *Ben Nevis* to Galveston Island. Passengers on the ship were struck with cholera even before reaching the Atlantic Ocean. When they arrived in Galveston, they faced another epidemic—yellow fever. The approximately four hundred fifty Wends who survived were then faced with a grueling 120-mile trip by ox cart from the coast to the area in Central Texas that is now Lee County near Giddings.

These early settlers were a thrifty, hard-working group who brought with them little more than a few tools, their religion, and their traditions. Soon after reaching where Serbin was to be, they built St. Paul's Lutheran Church and a school to exercise their American right to worship and educate their children as they chose. Later, when groups of Wends moved to other parts of the state, organizing a church and school took top priority. All of the Wendish churches built in Texas joined the fledgling Missouri Synod because of Reverend Kilian's relationship with the founders of that group.

To soften their otherwise difficult lives, the Wends continued to socialize and to maintain their cultural and religious celebrations. In the early years *Ptaci Kwas*, or the Wedding of the Birds, was celebrated every year on the eve of January 21. On this day children would place empty saucers or plates on fence posts, in a place where squirrels and other animals could not reach them. In the morning the plates would be filled with candies and other sweets, supposedly left by the birds. The children were told that during the night the birds celebrated their weddings and left the sweet offerings so the humans could share in their joy. Of course, it was not too long after that when, with the arrival of spring, the children noticed the freshly laid eggs in the nests and then saw baby birds trying to fly.

Today the only place the Wedding of the Birds is routinely celebrated is on the campus of Concordia University in Austin. Concordia University was founded by Jan Kilian, and even today a large percentage of the students are of Wendish heritage. The church bell that Reverend Kilian brought across the Atlantic Ocean on the "plague ship" is placed as a monument to the Wendish culture on the campus. Each year in January, the Wedding of the Birds is celebrated with children dressing up in bird costumes and acting out the ceremony. The celebration includes the jubilant "birds" passing out cookies to all the onlookers.

For her wedding, a Wendish bride traditionally wore a black dress with a white veil. After the wedding the veil was often hung over the marriage bed.

The black dress signified that the bride was leaving behind her carefree days of childhood and entering the world of marriage with the sorrows and heartbreak of adulthood. Later the black was softened to gray and then, by the turn of the century, brides were married in white like they are today. Some Wends today speculate that the real reason for the black dress was not the depressing official explanation. Rather, married women were required to wear black when taking communion and also for a year after a close relative died. Therefore, all married women needed a good black dress. Being thrifty and practical by nature, the bride married in a good black dress that she would surely need to wear often after her marriage.

The next major holiday of the year is Easter. Not only is this important in the church calendar, it is also a time to decorate the special Wendish Easter eggs. A design is applied to the egg with either a pin or feather dipped in beeswax. (Today the wax is often a mixture of paraffin and beeswax.) Then the egg is dipped into a colorful dye. This process can be repeated to create a more intricate pattern with several layers of wax and dye. Once the egg is dry it is wiped with a warm cloth to remove the wax and reveal the white shell beneath the design and to give the egg a festive shine.

Hard-boiled eggs were usually decorated quite simply because they were eaten almost as soon as the children found them in traditional egg hunts. The more intricately decorated eggs with many layers of wax and different dyes were given as special gifts to be kept and enjoyed for a long time. They were made from eggshells that had had the insides removed.

The noodle-makers today often blow the eggs from the shells so they can decorate them for either gifts or to sell at the festivals along with the noodles. Sometimes the eggs are blown in the traditional way—with a pinhole at each end and a lot of forceful breath. However, the modern Wend uses an especially developed egg syringe to aspirate the contents of the shell. According to one regular noodle-maker, this technique leaves only one small hole, the eggs are still usable, and it does not require the enormous lungpower of the traditional method!

The Wends, like other immigrant groups, seized every opportunity to gather for religious or social celebrations. On every occasion good food, music, singing, dancing, and beer helped make the festivities lively. Major events such as baptisms, weddings, and funerals often lasted three days. Although these days were filled with fun and camaraderie, there was also a practical side to the long celebrations. On the first day, the men slaughtered and began preparing the animals for the celebration. The women baked and prepared delicacies. Without refrigeration, everything had to be freshly prepared. The celebration generally took place on the second day. Then the third day was needed to recover and clean up after the event. Food was always a significant highlight of any gathering or celebration.

Today this tradition continues. Every September, the Wendish Heritage Museum in Serbin sponsors a Noodle Cook-Off and Wendish Festival with noodles, barbecue, music, singing, and beer. Sometimes Wends from Germany who are also interested in preserving the culture attend, delighting everyone with native dancing and costumes and by speaking the language with those who still remember it.

As with many cultures, Christmas was the largest celebration of the year. Young children lived in fear of *Rumplich* (also known as *Knect Ruprecht*), who would come to each house carrying a switch to whip bad children and a sack to carry away the worst boys. This scary creature generally wore a red suit with either a wide white or yellow stripe on the pants and jacket. On his face he wore a mask made from cloth with a beard made from the long hairs of a cow's tail. Sometimes the young men from the community who played *Rumplich* would tease the younger children by plotting with one of the more rambunctious boys to stuff him in the sack and take him away, scaring the little ones so much they would not dare misbehave the entire month of December!

Yet *Rumplich* prayed with the good children and brought special treats and toys for them. He also decorated the tree in the parlor of each home. Of course, the parents had actually decorated the tree earlier with fruits, nuts, and candies. Sometimes ribbons or special glass ornaments were also on the tree. After they decorated the tree, the parents would close the door to the parlor and forbid the children from entering. On Christmas Eve after church services, they were allowed in and the candles on the tree would be lit. Beneath the tree would be one or two simple, unwrapped gifts from *Rumplich* for each child. The glorious sight of the tree and all the gifts after so much anticipation and dread of *Rumplich* made each Christmas celebration memorable for the children.

The Wends are the only distinct cultural group to immigrate to Texas that did not first have their own country. That was why they came: to save their culture from the Germans who ruled them. Ironically, the Wends were greatly influenced by the German immigrants who came in even larger numbers and settled in the same areas. An example is St. Paul's Lutheran Church in Serbin, which has gone from having services solely in Wendish to having services in Wendish, German, and English every Sunday, to having services only in English and occasionally German. Except

for a few people who are attempting to revive the culture, Wendish is rarely spoken today, but many of the customs, traditions, and foods have been preserved.

Wendish Recipes

Though the Wends are very hard working and thrifty, they always enjoy plenty of tasty, hearty food. Whenever they gather to eat, the meal always begins and ends with a prayer.

Before the Meal:

> *Come Lord Jesus be our guest*
> *And let Thy gifts to us be blessed.*
>
> *Amen*

After the Meal:

> *Oh give thanks unto the Lord*
> *For He is good.*
> *And His mercy endureth forever.*
>
> *Amen*

Wobid—the noon meal:

The noon meal usually included a soup of meat broth with potatoes or noodles, vegetables, eggs, relishes, and bread. Noodles were (and still are) a mainstay of their diet.

Wendish Noodles

This is a variation of the traditional recipe used at the Texas Wendish Heritage Museum. It makes a dough that is easy to use when rolling and cutting by hand.

1 egg
3 tablespoons water (approximately half an egg shell)
1½ to 2 cups flour
Dash of salt

Beat egg and water together. Add salt and enough flour to form a stiff dough. Roll out about ¼ inch thick on a pastry cloth. Allow the pastry to dry slightly, turning occasionally. Cut into thin strips when dry but still pliable. Cook in chicken broth until tender.

Note: Chopped parsley, chopped green onion tops, and a dash of nutmeg may be added for flavor.

Sweet Noodles

Fresh, homemade noodles are always best, but if you need to save time and work, use dry, packaged noodles.

Noodle Recipe—cut the noodles but do not cook
2 cups milk
2 tablespoons sugar
Nutmeg or cinnamon

Heat the milk and sugar. Cook the noodles in this mixture for about 20 minutes. Sprinkle generously with grated nutmeg. Serve warm.

Meat

On Sundays or when guests were expected, the Wends loved to serve fresh roasted duck, chicken, goose, or some other kind of meat. At other times, meat was not usually served. When meats were stewed, the seasoned stock was used for boiling their homemade noodles or dumplings.

Country Meat Pie

Crust:

½ cup tomato sauce
½ cup bread crumbs
1 pound ground beef
¼ cup chopped onion
1¼ cups chopped green pepper
1 teaspoon salt
⅛ teaspoon oregano
⅛ teaspoon pepper

Mix well. Line the bottom and sides of a 9-inch pie pan with the meat mixture. Set aside and make filling.

Filling:

1½ cups Minute rice
1 cup water
½ cup tomato sauce
1 cup grated cheddar cheese
¼ teaspoon salt

Combine rice, tomato sauce, salt, water, and ¼ cup cheese. Spoon into meat crust. Cover with foil. Bake at 350° for 25 minutes. Uncover and sprinkle top with remaining cheese. Bake uncovered 10-15 minutes longer. Cut into wedges and serve. Makes 5-6 servings.

Four-Day Corned Beef

8 pounds brisket
3 cloves minced garlic
3 teaspoons saltpeter (purchase at a drug store)
4 tablespoons salt
2 tablespoons allspice
1 tablespoon sugar

Mix the last 5 ingredients together and rub into the brisket. Wrap in heavy foil and refrigerate for 4 days. Do not unwrap. Cook in foil 4 hours at 325°. Slice thinly across the grain and serve with dark bread and slaw.

Barbecue Sauce

Even today, the Wends serve noodles with barbecue—an interesting blending of old-world customs with traditional Texas ways.

2 cups chopped onion
¼ cup butter
¼ cup cooking oil
1 tablespoon vinegar
1 quart catsup
1 quart water
1 tablespoon brown sugar
½ teaspoon dry mustard
2 teaspoons celery seed
½ teaspoon paprika
1 tablespoon garlic powder
1 teaspoon onion powder
2 teaspoons chili powder
½ lemon, thinly sliced

½ cup chili sauce
1 tablespoon Louisiana hot sauce
1 tablespoon Worcestershire sauce

Brown the chopped onion lightly in butter. Add the remaining ingredients and simmer for two hours. Stir occasionally to prevent scorching. Serve hot over roasted meat.

Note: There are as many variations of this recipe as there are cooks! Adjust the ingredients to suit your own taste.

Kaltoffell Kloesa
(Potato Dumplings)

2   cups hot mashed potatoes
1   tablespoon butter
1   tablespoon minced onion
1   egg
¾   cup flour
1½ teaspoons salt
⅛   teaspoon pepper
4   slices toasted bread, cut into small cubes
2   quarts (8 cups) beef broth—homemade, canned, or instant

Blend the first seven ingredients together. Form a ball around 4 or 5 small toast cubes. Boil in beef broth about 9 to 10 minutes. Makes about 12 dumplings.

Hot Cabbage Slaw

Slaw:
1   large head of cabbage
1   teaspoon salt

Dressing:
1   slightly beaten egg
1   teaspoon salt
¼   cup vinegar
Dash of pepper

Finely shred the cabbage. Cook cabbage and salt in a covered pan over low heat until very tender. Mix all the ingredients for the dressing and pour over hot cabbage. Heat for 5 minutes. Serve immediately.

Cucumber Salad

2 medium green cucumbers
½ teaspoon salt
2 tablespoons sugar
2 tablespoons vinegar
2 tablespoons cream
⅛ teaspoon pepper

Peel and thinly slice the cucumbers, discarding the bitter ends. Put in a shallow dish and sprinkle with salt. Place a saucer on top of the cucumbers to weight them down. Set in a cool place for 30 minutes. Drain the cucumbers. Mix the sugar, vinegar, and cream and add to the cucumbers. Sprinkle with pepper. Serve immediately.

Wina Pliwka
(Wine Soup)

1 quart water
¼ cup tapioca
3 cinnamon sticks, broken into small pieces
4 slices lemon
⅓ cup sugar
1 cup wine
½ teaspoon vanilla
½ cup toasted bread cubes
¼ cup seedless raisins (optional)

Bring water to a boil. Add tapioca, cinnamon, lemon slices, and raisins. Cook until clear and raisins are plump. Remove from heat and add sugar, wine, and vanilla. Serve over toasted bread cubes.

Polievka
(Hamburger/Vegetable Soup)

2   quarts water
½   pound hamburger
1   onion, diced
1   cup diced carrots
2   teaspoons rice
1   small can tomatoes
1   tablespoon chopped parsley
1   cup diced celery
Salt and pepper to taste

Brown the crumbled hamburger. Drain. Slowly boil all the ingredients together for 1 hour.

Potato Pie

1   9-inch unbaked pie shell
3   eggs, separated
1   cup sugar
1   cup mashed potatoes
1   cup hot milk
1   tablespoon vanilla
Nutmeg
Meringue (optional)

Prebake pie shell for 10 minutes at 450°. Beat egg yolks until thick. Add sugar,

potatoes, hot milk, and vanilla. Mix well. Pour into pie shell and sprinkle the top with nutmeg. Bake at 350° for 30 minutes or until golden brown. Make meringue from egg whites and bake until it is golden (optional). Cool slightly before cutting.

Note: This is a delicious custard-type pie.

Coffee Cake

This coffee cake is still a favorite—either as a snack or dessert.

2 cups warm water
1 package rapid rise yeast
3 cups flour
1 cup sugar
¼ cup melted shortening
½ cup milk
½ teaspoon salt
3-4 cups flour
Topping

Mix together 2 cups of flour, sugar, salt, and yeast. Add warm water, shortening, and milk and mix together. Add as much flour as you need to make a smooth dough. Form into a ball, place in greased bowl, cover, and let rest for 10 minutes. Grease two cookie sheets and divide the dough. Spread the dough to the edges of the cookie sheets by hand. Cover and let dough rise to double in bulk. While the dough is rising, prepare the topping. Spread your choice of topping over the dough. Bake according to the directions for that topping.

Streusel Topping:
1 cup sugar
2 cups flour
¼ teaspoon salt
¼ cup butter or margarine
¼ cup melted shortening
Fruit (apples, pears, or other preserved fruit, as desired)
Cinnamon (optional)

Mix together flour, sugar, and salt. Add melted shortening and butter. Mix by hand until crumbly. Dot top of coffee cake with fruit. Sprinkle streusel topping over the fruit. Bake at 350° for 15-20 minutes or until brown. Sprinkle with cinnamon, if desired.

Cheese Topping:
1 small package lemon pie filling
½ cup water
1 egg
1½-2 cups dry cottage cheese
¾ cup sugar
¼ teaspoon lemon juice
Dash of salt
¼ cup melted butter or margarine
¼ cup sugar

Coffee Cake (Cont.)

Dissolve lemon pie filling in water. Add beaten egg and mix well. Add cottage cheese, salt, ¾ cup sugar, and lemon juice. Set aside. Bake plain coffee cake at 350° about 15-20 minutes or until streaks appear. Remove from oven, spread cheese mixture over top. Bake about 5 minutes more. Drizzle melted butter over top of coffee cake and sprinkle with ¼ cup sugar.

Molasses Taffy

A fun social event was the traditional taffy pull. Whole families would join in the fun of pulling the taffy and then eating the delicious results!

1½ cups sugar
½ cup molasses
2 tablespoons vinegar
½ teaspoon cream of tartar
4 tablespoons butter
¼ teaspoon salt
¼ teaspoon baking soda

Boil together the sugar, molasses, vinegar, and cream of tartar until mixture reaches medium crack stage (270°). Remove from heat and add butter, salt, and soda. When cool enough to handle, butter hands and pull the taffy until it is light in color. Pull or roll taffy into strips.

Note: ½ cup finely chopped nuts can be kneaded into the candy.

Pecan Macaroons

3   cups pecans, chopped very fine

2   cups brown sugar

3   egg whites

Mix pecans and brown sugar. Add egg whites. Mix well. Shape into small balls. Bake on a sprayed cookie sheet at 300° until lightly browned, about 10 minutes.

Easter Egg Dye

7   red or purple onions

7   eggs

Water

Drop the colored peelings from the onions into boiling water. Add the eggs. Boil for 7 minutes.

Note: After the colored eggs cool, they are ready to be decorated with wax.

Use yellow onions to make yellow eggs. Use more colored onions for more eggs and for a more intense color.

The Old and the New—
African Americans in Texas

Unlike most of the other people who came to Texas, most African Americans did not come by choice. They came with their owners from slave states. In spite of the Mexicans' opposition to slavery, Stephen F. Austin received permission for his settlers to bring slaves in his grant from the Mexican government. Once Texas became independent, free Blacks in Texas saw many changes in their status. The Mexican government had considered African Americans virtually as equal citizens, but without the right to hold office. The Republic of Texas did not protect Blacks in the same way. The Republic took away their citizenship and attempted to restrict their property rights.

When Texas was under Spanish and Mexican rule, slavery was not recognized. Freemen and thousands of runaway slaves from the United States came here seeking freedom. They were looking for a place to live without the fears and restrictions they faced in other states—basically the same reasons so many Europeans came to Texas beginning in the late 1800s.

By the time Texas became a state, slavery had become an important part of the economy, especially in East Texas. Here, the Southern system of large plantations worked by slave labor encouraged slavery. However, only about twenty-five percent of the families in Texas ever owned slaves. Freemen in Texas experienced a significant curtailment of their rights under statehood. One law a decade before the Civil War gave free Blacks two years to leave the state or be sold into slavery. This virtually stopped the movement of freemen into Texas.

At the start of the Civil War, Texas was definitely a slave state. Slaves not only worked the land but they also did the household work, including the cooking. So much of what is now considered "Southern cooking" was actually first created by the slaves who worked in their owners' kitchens. Here they had the best cuts of meat, fresh fruits and vegetables, and plenty of sugar and flour. With these ingredients they made delicious meals and treats for everyday consumption as well as for special events. Fried chicken, mashed potatoes, and fluffy biscuits have become Southern favorites.

Back in the slave quarters, a different situation existed. Here the slaves had to make hearty, filling meals with whatever they had. The meats were largely the organs and other undesirable cuts, supplemented by whatever wild animals they could kill on their own. Vegetables consisted of wild greens and the crops they could grow on their own—mainly such things as sweet potatoes and corn. Even after emancipation, the freemen often could not afford different foods. Here is where the biggest challenges existed—how to create delicious filling meals with whatever was available.

In spite of this shortage of supplies in the kitchen, the Black cooks became known for being able to create wonderful, tasty meals. In fact, even after emancipation, many former slaves continued to cook—either for their former masters for wages or in their own cafes and restaurants.

Juneteenth is to former Texas slaves what July 4th is to other Americans. It is liberation day. Every year, June nineteenth is a day of great celebration. On this day in 1865, word finally arrived in Texas that the slaves were free. However, the news

arrived two and a half years after the fact. The slave owners' explanation was that President Lincoln had sent the news by a courier who traveled from Washington by mule. In all likelihood, the slave owners knew about the signing of the Emancipation Proclamation, but refused to tell their slaves. Finally, the president had to send a squad of soldiers to free the over two hundred thousand slaves still in bondage in Texas. Once the proclamation was read in Galveston on June 19, 1865, the news spread quickly. Some former slaves dropped their tools and walked away from their jobs and former owners. Others continued to farm the land as sharecroppers rather than slaves. Regardless of what they did, they celebrated.

The first Juneteenth celebration was in the state capital in 1867 under the direction of the Freeman's Bureau. Just a couple of years later, the celebration became a part of the calendar of public events. To this day, Juneteenth is a day for celebration throughout the state. In fact, in recent times African Americans in other states have begun celebrating Juneteenth, even though their freedom came considerably earlier. Although this day is marked in a variety of ways, the celebrations usually revolve around outdoor activities in the normally mild June weather. Rodeos, baseball games, and dancing are a part of the celebration, but the center of the

festivities is always the barbecue pit. In early days, the celebrants dug a huge pit to roast a whole pig and whatever else they wanted to cook. Today, barbecue is still on the menu!

Because of the many hardships they faced in their everyday lives, the African Americans took advantage of every opportunity to have fun. Church has been one place where the Blacks have, at least since emancipation, been free. Prior to the Civil War, many Black churches were actually controlled by the landowners. After the Civil War, many Black Texans became Baptists. They liked the congregational organization that gave them local autonomy without a controlling organization above the congregation level. Finally, the slaves could be in control of their own worship. Methodist missionaries came to Texas from Northern states to organize the existing Black Methodist churches. Until recently most Blacks were either Baptist or Methodist. Beginning in the early twentieth century, more Blacks became involved in independent "holiness" churches. These churches fulfill the need for spiritual excitement often lacking in other denominations. Whether Baptist, Methodist, or independent, Black worship services are known for their lively, spontaneous atmosphere and the spectacular music. Gospel singing, a music category of its own, first began in Southern Black churches. The spirituals they sang expressed their faith in God. It continues to be extremely popular, not just in Black churches, but among all Christians.

Even chores such as cleaning the church grounds and cemeteries took on a festive atmosphere. Every family brought a clean sheet to use as a tablecloth for the groaning board laden with each woman's specialty. After all the weeds had been pulled and all the graves had been tended, the huge potluck picnic or "dinner on the grounds" was served. The children played games and the adults joined in or visited with each other.

As early as slave days, the time between Christmas and New Year's was a time for celebration for owners and slaves alike. Slaves took great care in selecting the yule log. As long as it still burned, the festive atmosphere continued. Since the crops had been harvested and sold, slaves had less work during this time. Gifts and special foods were usually given to the slaves. There were frequent visitors during this time, and they often rewarded those who helped them with coins or special treats. As a result, Christmas was a time of great celebration and rejoicing.

Today, Christmas is a combination of the religious and the secular. Santa Claus brings gifts to good children. In a recent effort to foster Black pride, he is sometimes portrayed as a Black man in a red suit.

Just as other ethnic groups have had a resurgence in cultural curiosity and pride, so have the African Americans. In the mid-1960s the Ethiopian holiday of Kwanza was introduced in the United States and Texas. Kwanza—the first fruits of harvest—is a traditional celebration that lasts for seven days from December 26 to January 1. This is not a religious holiday, nor is it one that honors a person or event. Instead it is a celebration of a people, a time for honoring the past, present, and future of African Americans.

Kwanza established a set of goals called the *Nguzo Saba* that everyone, especially children, is to memorize. The seven goals are a framework for behavior and actions throughout the entire year. They are designed to nurture pride in their heritage and to encourage actions to improve one's self and community.

One candle is lit each day of Kwanza to symbolize one of the seven principles that can help Blacks take charge of their lives. These principles are:

1) Unity—of the family, community, nation, and race.

2) Self-determination—defining oneself instead of being defined by others.

3) Collective work and responsibility—working together to solve problems.

4) Cooperative economics—helping and supporting each other to build and maintain businesses.

5) Purpose—to restore all Blacks to their traditional greatness by building and developing the community.

6) Creativity—improving the community to make it more beautiful and beneficial to all.

7) Faith—to believe in parents, teachers, the Black people, and the righteousness and victory of the struggle.

During the celebration of Kwanza, Blacks fast during the day. At sunset they break the fast. Decorations for Kwanza use the symbolic colors of red to represent the blood of ancestors, black to represent the race, and green to represent land, youth, the future, and the reason to continue. Parents teach their children about their heritage and end the week of celebration by giving them educational gifts such as books on the last day, January 1, when the last candle is lit.

African American couples today are incorporating African traditions into their marriage ceremonies. This includes the use of *adinkra* cloth in the wedding attire. The word "adinkra" means good-bye. Originally royalty wore the cloth for mourning during funeral services. Today *adinkra* cloths are used for special occasions such as weddings and other important events. Stylized symbols with special meaning decorate the cloth. The motifs and their meaning are derived from a proverb, historical event, human attitude, or something else important. The *adinkra* symbol on

page 142 represents the omnipotence of God. Other symbols appropriate for weddings represent such concepts as love, devotion, faithfulness, etc.

Jumping the broom is a tradition that represents the sweeping away of the old and the welcoming of the new. It is the symbol of a new beginning. During slave days, the broom jumping ritual honored the creation of the new union between a man and a woman because marriage between slaves was not allowed. Today it relates to the joining of the couple as well as the combining of the two families. It includes the need for the community to support the newly married couple.

Today, as in the past, family and tradition play an important role in the lives of Texas' African Americans. Whenever family and friends gather, wonderful food is always an important ingredient.

African American Recipes

Corn Bread

1¾ cups cornmeal
1 teaspoon baking powder
1 teaspoon baking soda
½ teaspoon salt
2 cups buttermilk
1 egg
3 tablespoons shortening

Preheat the oven to 450°. Heat the shortening in a 9-inch iron skillet. Mix the dry ingredients together. Mix the egg and buttermilk together. Combine the dry and liquid ingredients. When the shortening starts to smoke a little, pour most but not all into the batter. Mix well. Pour the batter into the hot skillet with the rest of the shortening in it. Bake in the middle of the preheated oven for 30 minutes until brown on top.

Note: Cooking oil, bacon grease, melted butter, or margarine can be used for shortening. Serve with butter, pinto beans, and greens. For a special treat, pour molasses or honey over the corn bread.

Buttermilk Biscuits

For holidays, try using a simple cookie cutter instead of a round biscuit cutter. Make hearts for Valentine's Day, pumpkins or bats at Halloween, and bells at Christmas.

2 cups flour
2½ teaspoons baking powder
½ teaspoon salt
⅓ cup shortening
¾ cup buttermilk

Mix together flour, baking powder, and salt. Cut in shortening with a fork until the mixture resembles coarse cornmeal. Add buttermilk. Blend lightly until the dough pulls away from the sides of the bowl. Knead lightly (about 30 seconds). Roll ¾ inch thick. Cut with a biscuit cutter, dipping it into flour between each cut. Place on a lightly greased or sprayed pan. Brush the tops of the biscuits with butter or margarine. Bake at 475° for 12 to 15 minutes.

Note: If you do not have any buttermilk, mix together ¾ cup milk and the juice (no pulp) from one lemon. Or you can use powdered buttermilk. Either makes tasty biscuits!

 GYE NYAME (except God)
Symbol of the OMNIPOTENCE OF GOD
Proverb
Abode santan yi firi tete: obi nte ase a onim n'ahyase, na obi ntena ase nkosi n'awie, Gye Nyame.
(This Great Panorama of creation dates back to time immemorial, no one lives who saw its beginning, no one will live to see its end, Except God.)

Hushpuppies

According to tradition, these tasty corn bread balls were tossed to the dogs to keep them quiet during meals. At my house there are never enough for both the humans and the pets to eat!

1	cup cornmeal
½	cup flour
½	teaspoon salt
1	teaspoon sugar
½	teaspoon baking powder
½	teaspoon baking soda
½	teaspoon garlic powder
½	teaspoon pepper
1	tablespoon dried, minced onion
1	egg, slightly beaten
1	cup milk
2	cups vegetable oil

Combine dry ingredients including onion. Stir in the egg. Slowly add the milk until the batter is thick but will still drop easily from a spoon. You may not need all the milk. Heat the oil in a skillet. Drop the batter by teaspoonfuls into the hot oil and fry until golden brown. Serve hot.

Note: Bacon fat can be substituted for the oil. Two tablespoons minced scallions can be substituted for the dried onion.

Spoon Bread

Spoon bread got its name because you "spoon" it onto your plate rather than slicing it like regular bread. It is really a cornmeal soufflé!

2	cups milk
½	cup cornmeal
1	teaspoon salt
2	tablespoons butter or margarine
½	teaspoon baking powder
2	eggs, separated

Put a greased 2-quart baking dish in an oven heated to 400°. Boil the milk. Gradually stir in the cornmeal. The mixture will be stiff. Add the salt and butter. Remove from the heat and add the baking powder. Add beaten egg yolks to the batter. Beat the egg whites until they are stiff. Fold the egg whites into the batter. Pour the batter into the hot, greased baking dish. Bake for 35-40 minutes until it is firm in the middle and brown on top. Serve immediately.

Note: For variety, add one of the following: 1 cup mixed frozen diced vegetables, 1 cup shredded cheese, or 4 slices crumbled, crisp bacon.

Short'nin' Bread

Every child has sung the song about short'nin' bread, and this recipe is so easy a child can make it!

2	cups flour
½	cup sugar, brown or white
1	cup butter or margarine at room temperature

Mix all the ingredients until they form a soft dough. Roll or pat until the dough is about ½ inch thick. Cut with a biscuit cutter. Bake on lightly greased or sprayed cookie sheet at 350° for 25-30 minutes.

Note: Try adding a little cinnamon to these. Yum!

Grits and Cheese

1½ cups quick grits

1 teaspoon garlic salt

1 teaspoon savory salt

6 cups water

¾ cup butter or margarine

4 eggs, well beaten

8 drops Tabasco sauce (more or less, to taste)

1 pound grated cheddar cheese

Paprika for garnish

Boil water, garlic salt, and savory salt. Slowly stir in grits and cook for 5 minutes, stirring occasionally. Remove from heat and stir in butter. Mix together the eggs, Tabasco, and cheese. Add the egg mixture to the hot grits. Pour into a large greased or sprayed baking dish. Sprinkle with paprika. Bake at 250° for one hour until a knife inserted in the center comes out clean. Serve hot.

Hoppin' John

1 cup dried black-eyed peas

¼ pound salt pork, diced

1 chopped green pepper

1 chopped onion

2 cups cooked rice

1 tablespoon butter or margarine

Tabasco, to taste

Soak peas overnight in 3 cups of water. Drain. In a large pan combine the peas, pork, green pepper, and onion. Cover with water and simmer for about 2 hours until peas are tender. Add the remaining ingredients. Cover and cook very slowly until all the liquid is absorbed. Serve hot.

Note: Great with corn bread!

Kwanza Blessing Soup

1　chicken, about 3 pounds

½　teaspoon salt

1　teaspoon pepper

¼　teaspoon red pepper flakes

1　medium onion, chopped

2　teaspoons chopped parsley

6　cups water

2　teaspoons vegetable oil

4　sweet potatoes, peeled and cut into cubes

Put everything in a pot, except the sweet potatoes. Bring to a boil then lower the heat. Add the sweet potatoes, cover, and simmer until the chicken is tender, about 40-50 minutes. Place the chicken on a serving platter and surround it with the sweet potatoes.

Greens

1　pound greens—collard, kale, mustard or turnip greens, or a mixture of any of them

1　package smoked turkey necks or wings

Boil turkey necks for 25-30 minutes in a large pot filled halfway with water. Wash the greens several times in cold water until they are no longer gritty and water runs clear. Remove any thick stems or veins from the leaves. Cut greens into pieces and place in the pot of boiling water with the turkey. Cook until tender.

Note: Serve with fried chicken and macaroni and cheese for a hearty meal.

Fried Green Tomatoes

4   green tomatoes
½   teaspoon salt
½   teaspoon pepper
½   teaspoon garlic powder
¾   cup flour
2   eggs, beaten
4   tablespoons butter or margarine

Slice the green tomatoes ½ inch thick. Mix the flour and seasonings. Dredge the tomato slices in flour, dip in beaten eggs, then back in flour. Melt the butter in a skillet. Sauté the tomato slices until golden brown, about 3-5 minutes on each side.

Fried Yams

½   cup cooking oil
3   yams or sweet potatoes, washed and thinly sliced
1   cup sugar
½   teaspoon nutmeg
2   tablespoons butter or margarine
3   tablespoons lemon juice

Fry the yams in the oil until they are golden brown. Mix the sugar, nutmeg, butter, and lemon juice and heat until the butter is melted. Pour the warm sauce over the fried potatoes. Serve warm.

Note: To save calories and fat, oven fry the sweet potatoes. Place the potato slices on a sprayed cookie sheet. Spray the potatoes. Bake at 400° for about 10 minutes until golden.

Fried Corn

2 cups whole kernel fresh corn
1 diced green pepper
½ cup flour
1 tablespoon sugar
Salt and pepper to taste
½ cup butter or margarine

Shuck and de-silk the corn, then rinse. With a sharp knife, cut the kernels of corn from the cob. Mix in green pepper, flour, sugar, salt, and pepper. Heat the butter or margarine. Fry the corn mixture until the corn is tender and the flour starts to brown. Stir frequently to prevent the flour from sticking.

Note: Frozen or canned corn can be used.

Candied Sweet Potatoes

Try these and you will never put marshmallows on your sweet potatoes again!

4 large sweet potatoes
2 cups white sugar
8 tablespoons (1 stick) butter or margarine
2 teaspoons vanilla
2 teaspoons bourbon (optional)
Dash of nutmeg and/or cinnamon

Peel and slice the potatoes. Rinse well, then dry. Put the potatoes in a pot and pour all the other ingredients over them. Cover with a tight-fitting lid. Simmer for 45 minutes to an hour until the potatoes are tender and a syrup forms.

Note: Canned sweet potatoes can be used instead of fresh.

Oven-Barbecued Baby Beef Ribs

2   pounds baby beef ribs
4   chopped green onions
2   teaspoons butter or margarine
1   teaspoon flour
1   teaspoon dried mustard
1   cup beef broth
2   teaspoons lemon juice
3   teaspoons chili sauce
Freshly ground black pepper to taste

Place ribs in a single layer in a shallow roasting pan. Bake at 350° for 20 to 30 minutes. Drain the fat.

Barbecue Sauce:

Sauté the onion in the butter until tender. Add the flour and mix well. Stir in broth, mustard, lemon juice, chili sauce, and pepper. Cook 5 to 7 minutes until sauce is smooth and thick.

Brush the sauce over the ribs. Bake another 30 minutes until tender, basting occasionally with the sauce.

Ham Steak and Red-Eye Gravy

Once considered a breakfast treat, ham and red-eye gravy is a hearty meal any time of the day! Serve with greens and grits for some great eating.

1   slice ham, about a half inch thick
1   tablespoon vegetable oil
¾   cup water
2   tablespoons strong, black coffee

Soak the ham in cold water for 45 minutes to remove the salt (optional). Drain and dry the ham. Heat the vegetable oil in a heavy skillet until it is hot but not smoking. Cook the ham, turning occasionally, until it is tender, about 20 minutes. Put the ham steak on a serving plate and keep warm.

Gravy:

Boil the water in the skillet, stirring to loosen all the brown bits in the pan. Boil 5 minutes. Add the coffee to darken the gravy. Add a little more water if the gravy is too thick. Pour over ham steak and serve immediately.

Southern Fried Chicken

Someone always brings Southern fried chicken to a dinner on the grounds. It is a perennial favorite.

An African American kitchen always had a cast-iron skillet that was used for everything! If you have one, use it for this recipe.

2-3 pounds chicken cut into serving pieces
3-4 cups milk
½ teaspoon Tabasco sauce (optional)
1½ cups flour
½ teaspoon salt
½ teaspoon pepper
1 teaspoon paprika
1 teaspoon garlic powder
1 teaspoon poultry seasoning
2 cups vegetable oil

Put the chicken in a large bowl and add milk to cover. Add Tabasco sauce, if desired, and refrigerate for 1 hour. Combine the flour and seasonings in a heavy paper bag or a large plastic bag and shake to mix. Shake the excess milk off each piece of chicken as you take it out of the bowl. Drop the chicken, one piece at a time, into the bag of seasoned flour. Shake until well coated. In a large heavy skillet, heat the oil until flour sizzles when sprinkled on top. Reduce the heat a little and cook the chicken until golden brown, about 25-30 minutes. Drain.

Note: Do not let the pieces of chicken touch when you are browning them. Unless your skillet is huge, you will probably have to fry the chicken in batches. Use the leftover seasoned flour and milk from the chicken to make gravy.

If desired, add 2 tablespoons butter or margarine to the frying oil.

Sweet Potato Pie

This may look like pumpkin pie, but it tastes nothing like it! (Most tasters think sweet potato pie is better!)

1 can (29 oz.) sweet potatoes, drained

1¼ cups sugar

1 teaspoon lemon extract

1 tablespoon vanilla

1 teaspoon nutmeg

3 eggs

1 tablespoon milk or cream

6 tablespoons butter or margarine, melted

1 teaspoon flour

At medium speed mix all ingredients until smooth. Spoon the filling into an unbaked 9-inch pie shell. Bake at 350° for 1 hour or until firm.

Serve warm or cooled, with a little whipped cream on top.

Note: I like to use a frozen deep-dish pie shell.

Molasses Nog

2 cups evaporated milk

2 cups ice-cold water

2 tablespoons molasses

Ground nutmeg, ginger, or cinnamon to taste (optional)

Mix the milk, water, and molasses together until well blended. Pour into glasses. Sprinkle with the spice of your choice.

Peach Cobbler

The wonderful taste and aroma make you especially glad that this cobbler feeds a crowd!

3   cans (15 oz. each) sliced peaches, drained
1¾ cups sugar
1¾ teaspoons cinnamon
⅔   cup water
¾   cup (1½ sticks) butter or margarine
2   teaspoons lemon juice
¼   cup flour
Pastry for 3 9-inch pies

Heat the peaches, sugar, cinnamon, water, butter, and lemon juice until the butter is melted and the peaches are warm.

In a cup, mix the flour with some of the warm liquid from the pan. Stir until smooth. Stir the flour mixture into the peaches.

Put pastry on the bottom of a lightly buttered or sprayed 9x13-inch baking dish.

This will take about 2 pastries. Either weave a lattice with the remaining pastry or cut into shapes. Pour the peaches into the baking dish. Place the lattice or pastry shapes over the peaches. Bake at 350° for 35-40 minutes until the top is brown and the peaches are bubbling.

Note: If you prefer, you can use 8 cups of peeled, pitted, and sliced fresh peaches. Whichever you use, feel free to adjust the sugar and cinnamon to taste.

I like to use frozen deep-dish pie shells. Let them stand at room temperature for a few minutes to defrost. Just dampen your fingers to seal any holes or tears in the pastry.

Danes on the Prairie—

The Danes in Texas

June fifth—Independence Day

Young Myrtle Hansen chose this date in 1934 for her marriage so that every year there would be a celebration on her anniversary. Her parents, Niels and Emma Hansen, were among the immigrants who settled in Danevang, Texas, during the 1890s. The new Americans continued celebrating the day King Frederik VII signed Denmark's first free constitution, just as they had before they left Denmark to seek their fortunes in America. June fifth was a time to sing, dance, play games, and enjoy the camaraderie of friends and relatives. Myrtle, like others in the first generation born in Texas, continued this tradition of honoring her Danish heritage.

Of course, over time the celebration was no longer one demonstrating loyalty to a country an ocean away, but rather one of remembering the roots of those who had the courage and foresight to come to Texas. Today the June celebration is held on a weekend even if it is not the fifth of the month; the games are more likely to be bridge and dominoes instead of the more vigorous games of an earlier generation;

the Danish dancing is more likely to be in the form of an exhibition by a group from the Danish Historical Society of Houston or San Antonio; and children are likely enjoying building with the twentieth-century Danish invention Legos, which appropriately translates to "play good." Yet a celebration is still held each June with friends and relatives gathering at the meeting house, just as the first settlers had gathered over a century ago.

The name Danevang translates to "flat country settled by Danes," or "Danish meadow," an accurate description of the land. The flat land the advance team of Danes first saw stretched for miles. There were no trees except for a few scrub oaks growing along the banks of the Tres Palacious Creek. There were no roads or drainage ditches, so whenever it rained, the land flooded. Yet it was rich land and cheap, just what they were looking for.

A smattering of Danes had come to Texas prior to the establishment of

Danevang; at least one Dane died at the Alamo. The *Dansk Folkesamfund*, or Danish Folk Society, organized the sale of land to Danes in Wharton County, the first and largest Danish colony in Texas. Several of the early settlers were bachelors who first went to other areas of the United States where large numbers of Danes had settled. Railroad jobs brought them to Texas where they discovered fertile black land and a chance for prosperity and the ability to support wives and families that did not exist for them elsewhere.

They bought the land for one dollar down and a dollar a year for each acre for nine years. The total price per acre was nine dollars. No payment was due the first year. Even with these favorable terms, payments could not be made the first years. The black gumbo soil initially resisted cultivation. Then the Danish farmers tried to grow oats, corn, and grains as the Danes in the Midwest had, but these crops did not do well in this part of Texas. In addition, they were plagued with floods from heavy rains and then from the Galveston hurricane of 1900; an epidemic that killed most of their horses, mules, and cattle; and insects, crop failures, and a local depression. Many wanted to leave the colony but found that without funds, even that was impossible. The only alternative was to continue their tradition of hard work.

Concerned about the lack of payments, the land seller made several excursions from Chicago to the area. He was so impressed with the hard work and perseverance of the Danes in spite of the adverse conditions, that he decided not to foreclose. Within a few years the Danish immigrants had largely switched to cotton as the cash crop and had created a thriving community with neat houses and prosperous fields.

In the Danish tradition, the community members started schools, reading clubs, an insurance company, a telephone service, a grocery, a cotton gin, and a gasoline station, all on a cooperative basis similar to those they had known in Denmark. The schools taught biblical history, Danish history, and the Danish language, along with the regular "American" curriculum, at least until incorporation and state laws took over the community schools. Then these special classes continued in the summers for a number of years after the school and church had converted to the English language. Traditional Danish folk dancing continued to be taught to the young people in the community well into the second half of the twentieth century.

Like many groups that settled in Texas in the late nineteenth century, social life revolved largely around the church. The congregation of the Ansgar Evangelical Lutheran Church was founded in 1895, but it was over ten years before a church building was constructed. Unlike in Demark where both the schools and the church were

supported by the government, the original colonists discovered that they had to finance the building of a church and pay the pastor's salary themselves. Despite the economic hardships, the congregation voted to support a pastor. Services were held in homes until the meeting house was built.

The meeting house was the main gathering place for worship and gatherings of all types. Not only were worship services held there when there was no church, but the building was also used as a school, gymnasium, social hall, and roller skating rink. But every year around Christmas, the meeting house is the site of a uniquely Danish celebration.

In the center of the large main room stands an evergreen tree that towers towards the distant ceiling. Ornaments on the tree include strings of Danish and American flags, woven red and white heart-shaped baskets and cones, and other traditional decorations similar to those that decorated the trees of the early settlers. In the colonial days of Danevang, most Christmas trees also had paper cones filled with candies and the lights were candles rather than strings of electric tree lights.

As children enter the hall, they immediately gasp at the wonders of the tree. Often it is the largest one they have ever seen. This was the reaction of the children in early Danevang—the tree was a wondrous sight and they were filled with anticipation. Immediately everyone joins hands to form concentric circles. Circling

in alternating directions around the tree, everyone from toddlers just learning to walk to great-grandparents join in singing Christmas carols and dancing around the tree. The last song is always *Nu har Ve Jul Igen*, a traditional Danish tune that means, "Now Christmas is here again." The revelers stomp around the tree slowly the first time the song is sung and then as rapidly as possible the second time. Then everyone changes directions and does it again. After several choruses, children are laughing from tripping over their feet and falling on the floor, and the adults are likewise laughing and bumping into each other in a mass of hilarious confusion.

Santa Claus, the American version of the Danish Christmas elf *Nisse*, rescues the dancers by making his appearance with a huge sack over his shoulder. He takes his place in a special chair on the stage and invites the children to come to him, one at a time, to receive a bag filled with fruit, candy, and nuts, the same treats their parents, grandparents, and great-grandparents received as children. Then a Danish smorgasbord or buffet is served and everyone leaves, well fed and happy.

Visitors from Denmark who join in the Danevang version of a Danish Christmas usually end up laughing and shaking their heads in disbelief. What they see is Christmas as it was celebrated in Denmark over a century ago. Singing *Nu har Ve Jul Igen* and dancing around the tree is rarely, if ever, done in Denmark anymore! Then if the visitor tries to speak Danish with one of the old-timers who grew up speaking the language, he hears a form of the language that has not changed in over a century. Largely isolated from the rest of Danish culture, the language and customs in Danevang have not evolved in the last century as they have in Denmark.

Typically, Danish families celebrate on Christmas Eve by attending church services and then gathering with all the relatives at home. Dinner once featured a goose, but today a turkey is usually substituted. Dessert includes various pastries and rice pudding with an almond. Whoever receives the almond wins a small prize. Another version is that the person who finds the almond is supposed to be lucky in the coming year. Home celebrations, like the huge community one, include the singing of carols and the dancing around the tree while singing *Nu har Ve Jul Igen* before the opening of the gifts.

The first Danevang church was built in 1908. After several years of good crops, most farmers pledged four dollars per bale of cotton harvested to finance the cost of building it. Unfortunately, a hurricane in 1945 destroyed the building. At the end of World War II, it was replaced with the current building—a surplus chapel from Camp Hulen in Palacious, forty miles away. The new church, like other Danish churches, follows the Viking custom of hanging a model of a fully rigged sailing ship inside the sanctuary. The Danish consul from Houston presented the ship and a Danish flag to the church and community at its centennial celebration in 1994.

Danes are known for their calm disposition and ability to adapt to their surroundings. These attributes helped the early settlers assimilate into the Texas melting pot to become Americans. Although many of the descendants of the original colonists have moved away as farms have been consolidated into larger, more economical enterprises, the Danish heritage continues through the various Danish historical societies throughout the state.

Danish Recipes

"Tak for mad!" Thanks for the food!
"Velbekomme!" May it become you well!

Danish cooks pride themselves on a well-laid table. Traditional Danish cooking requires time and patience, but the results are worth it!

Frikadeller
(Danish Meatballs)

2½ pounds lean, finely ground pork
1 cup flour
2 tablespoons grated onion
2 teaspoons salt
1½ teaspoons pepper
3 eggs, slightly beaten
1½ cups low-fat milk
2 tablespoons butter or margarine

Blend the pork, flour, onion, salt, and pepper. Add the eggs. Add the milk ½ cup at a time, letting the mixture rest a few minutes between each addition so it will absorb all the milk. Beat with a spoon until almost fluffy. Chill at least 1 hour.

Heat 2 tablespoons butter in a large skillet over medium heat until it begins to brown. Roll the meat into walnut-size balls and fry until brown on all sides. Add more butter as needed. Bake at 250° for 20 minutes. Makes six servings.

Note: Ask the butcher to finely grind the meat for you or use the food processor.

You may substitute finely ground beef or veal for half of the pork.

Stegt And
(Roast Goose)

10 pound goose
Salt and pepper
4 cups boiling water

Season the goose inside and out with the salt and pepper. Put the goose in a large, deep pan. Bake at 425° for 20 minutes, then reduce the temperature to 325°. Add the water and baste. Roast for 3 hours. For a crisp skin, pour 2 tablespoons water over the goose and brown for 15 minutes more.

For gravy, skim off the fat from the drippings and add cornstarch or flour to thicken.

Note: The goose may be stuffed with peeled apple slices and prunes, if desired. Serve with red cabbage, browned potatoes, and a green salad for a holiday celebration.

Danish Meatloaf

1 pound ground beef
½ pound ground pork
1 egg, slightly beaten
1 medium onion, grated
1 teaspoon seasoned salt
¼ teaspoon pepper
¼ teaspoon nutmeg
¼ teaspoon allspice
¼ cup flour
½ cup milk

Grind the beef and pork together in your food processor. Add the egg, onion, and seasonings into the food processor.

Add the flour and process until well blended and fluffy. Slowly add the milk to the mixture while the processor is on. The meat mixture will be like a thick dough. Shape into a long loaf in a baking pan. Bake uncovered at 350° for one hour. Refrigerate the leftovers and slice when cold for the best meatloaf sandwiches you've ever eaten!

Note: You can use an electric mixer instead of a food processor.

Rodkal
(Red Cabbage)

This has always been a favorite at community dinners in Danevang!

1 medium head red cabbage, shredded
½ cup cooking oil
4 tablespoons sugar
4 tablespoons vinegar
Salt to taste

Heat the oil in a heavy skillet. Add sugar. When the sugar begins to brown, add cabbage and cover. Cook over medium heat for 30 minutes, stirring occasionally. Add the vinegar and salt to taste. Serve while still hot.

Note: Butter or margarine can be substituted for the cooking oil.

Brunde Kartofler
(Browned Potatoes)

2 or 3 cups cold boiled potatoes, cubed
1½ sticks (12 tablespoons) butter or
    margarine
2-3 tablespoons sugar

Melt the margarine in a skillet. Add potatoes and stir. Sprinkle with sugar. Cook, stirring often, until browned and a little caramelized. Serve warm.

Agurkesalat
(Cucumber Salad)

2   cups peeled cucumbers, thinly sliced

2   tablespoons salt

½   cup white vinegar

½   cup sugar

Soak the cucumbers and salt in just enough water to cover for an hour. Squeeze out the water. Heat the vinegar just enough to dissolve the sugar. Pour over cucumbers and chill. Serve cold and crisp.

Note: A few tablespoons of water may be added to the vinegar to dilute it when dissolving the sugar.

Rod Grod
(Fruit Soup)

1   quart sweetened fruit juice (grape, cherry, etc.)

½   cup tapioca (more or less depending on desired thickness)

Cinnamon or peppermint sticks (optional)

Bring juice to a boil. Add tapioca while stirring. Simmer until thickened. Cool. Stir each serving with a cinnamon or peppermint stick (optional).

Note: Served warm, this makes a wonderful snack on cold days. On warm days, serve cold soup with a scoop of ice cream on top. Delicious and very easy to make!

Powdered Sugar Icing

1   pound sifted powdered sugar

1   teaspoon almond flavoring or vanilla

Dash of salt

Milk

Mix the sugar, flavoring, and salt. Add milk, a few drops at a time, until it reaches the desired consistency. This icing should be thick.

Danish Puff

My cousin who lives in Ringstead, Denmark, served this to me when I visited her in her home. However, she had bought hers at the bakery. If she had realized how easy it is to make, she could have baked it herself!

First Layer:
- 1   cup flour
- 1   stick (8 tablespoons) butter or margarine
- 3   tablespoons water

Combine the flour and margarine as for a piecrust. Sprinkle with water and mix with a fork. Round into a ball and then divide into half. Pat the dough into 2 long strips about 12 x 3 inches on an ungreased cookie sheet.

Top Layer:
- 1   cup water
- 1   stick (8 tablespoons) butter or margarine
- 1   teaspoon almond flavoring
- 1   cup flour
- 3   eggs

Boil the water and margarine. Add the almond flavoring. Remove from heat. Stir in the flour until smooth. Add the eggs one at a time, beating until smooth after each addition. Spread half the mixture over each pastry strip. Bake 60 minutes at 350° until the top is crisp and brown. (Each strip will sound hollow when you tap the top.)

Frost with powdered sugar icing (page 160) using almond flavoring. Sprinkle with chopped nuts or toasted almonds.

Note: This recipe can be doubled.

My mother, who has the reputation for making the best Danish Puff in Danevang, always bakes hers the day she is to serve it. Although it is definitely best the day it is made, it is still good the next day, also.

Braided Kaffekage
(Braided Coffee Cake)

2   packages rapid rise yeast

½   cup warm water

1½ cups lukewarm milk (scald milk then cool to lukewarm)

½   cup sugar

2   teaspoons salt

2   eggs

½   cup soft shortening

7-7½ cups flour

1   stick (8 tablespoons) softened butter or margarine

Mix 6 cups flour, sugar, salt, and yeast in a large bowl. Heat milk, water, and shortening until very warm (about 120°-130°). Stir the liquids into the flour mixture. Stir in eggs. Add enough of the remaining flour to make a dough. Knead until smooth and elastic on a lightly floured surface. Smooth dough with your hands or with a rolling pin into a large, thick rectangle and thickly spread with butter or margarine. Fold ends over the buttered side and repeat until all the butter has been used. Roll up dough in a ball, cover, and let rest for 10 minutes.

Divide dough into 3 or 4 pieces. Using a rolling pin, form a rectangle about ½ inch thick and 5 inches wide. Cut into 3 long strips. Braid the strips, being sure to pinch the top and bottom securely. Repeat with each piece of dough. Let rise on cookie sheet until double in size. Bake at 350° degrees for about 15-20 minutes, until golden brown.

Decorate with powdered sugar icing, nuts, and sliced maraschino cherries as desired.

Note: The dough can be frozen during the resting period to be used at another time. Or it can be refrigerated for a few days before shaping and baking. Be sure to lightly oil the surface of the dough and to wrap it tightly. Bring it to room temperature before handling.

Although this recipe may seem like a lot of work, the number of delicious coffee cakes that it makes are worth the effort.

Kransekage
(Traditional Danish Wedding Cake)

A kransekage is an 18-layer cake that is really more like a cookie or pastry than a cake. It is only made for very special occasions, such as weddings or Independence Day. It is traditionally decorated with Danish flags or Danish and American flags in Texas. For weddings, the cake may be decorated with white doves. Sometimes a bottle of wine for the bridal couple is placed inside the kransekage.

1½ pounds almond paste
1½ cups sugar
3   egg whites, slightly beaten
Powdered sugar icing

Crumble the almond paste. Mix the almond paste, sugar, and egg whites thoroughly.

Use a cookie press to fill the 18 rings in *kransekage* ring pans.

OR

Cut brown paper into circles with the largest being 15" in diameter. Each circle should be about ½" smaller than the one before. Use the paper circles as guides for making the rings.

Bake the rings at 300° for 20 minutes or until lightly brown.

Using a cake decorating tube filled with powdered sugar icing (see page 160), pipe a thin line between the layers to hold them together. Starting at the top, make several rows of scallops from the icing around the cake. Decorate with Danish or American flags, doves, or slices of maraschino cherries and toasted almonds.

Note: This cake makes a very impressive presentation. But to make a delicious almond cookie for eating, bake the *kransekage* in strips rather than circles. After baking the dough, cut into slices.

Aebleskiver
(Pancake Balls)

This is a quick, easy version of a more complicated traditional recipe. Children love them!

4   cups biscuit mix
3   cups milk
4   eggs
¾   cup oil

Mix the biscuit mix, milk, and eggs, being careful not to stir too much. Heat 1 teaspoon oil in each hole of a monk's pan. Fill each hole half full with batter. When lightly browned, turn slowly. (A fondue fork or skewer works well for turning.) When done, a fork or toothpick comes out clean. Add oil as needed to the monk's pan. Sprinkle with sifted powdered sugar or serve plain with applesauce, syrup, jelly, or peanut butter.

Note: A monk's pan has seven round holes. It can be found at specialty stores.

Aeblekage
(Danish Apple Cake)

This is not really a cake, but it is a family favorite.

1   quart thick sweetened applesauce
1   teaspoon vanilla
1   cup or more graham cracker crumbs
½   teaspoon cinnamon
Whipped cream (or low-fat substitute)
Cherries or toasted almonds (optional)

Mix the vanilla and applesauce. Mix crumbs and cinnamon. Put a thin layer of crumbs on the bottom of the serving bowl. Alternate layers of applesauce and crumbs, ending with the applesauce. Top with whipped cream. Decorate with cherries or toasted almonds, if desired.

Note: This is extremely quick and easy to make. It tastes delicious and freezes beautifully. It is especially impressive when prepared in a clear glass bowl that shows off the layers.

Ris a la Mande
(Rice Almond Christmas Pudding)

4   cups milk
1½ cups rice
1   package unflavored gelatin
¼   cup cold water
¾   cup hot water
½   cup sugar
2   teaspoons vanilla
1   cup whipping cream or 8 oz. frozen
     whipped topping
1   almond

Bring the milk to a boil and add rice. Simmer until the rice is tender, about 20 minutes. Cool. Soften gelatin in the cold water, then add the hot water. Add the dissolved gelatin, sugar, and vanilla to the rice. Whip the cream or defrost the topping. Fold the whipped cream or topping into the rice mixture. Stir in the almond.

Serve in individual bowls with a spoonful of fruit soup, jelly, or canned pie filling on top.

Note: Whoever gets the bowl with the almond will have good luck during the coming year or perhaps win a small prize. Be sure to chew the pudding thoroughly or you may accidentally swallow the almond without realizing it! A definite sign of bad luck!

Pebbernodder
(Peppernuts)

This is the traditional treat to give to Christmas carolers who come by on a cold December night. The Germans have a very similar cookie that they also enjoy during the holidays.

1   cup butter
1½ cups brown sugar, packed
1   egg yolk
4   tablespoons cream
1   teaspoon cinnamon
¼   teaspoon ginger
3   cups flour
⅛   teaspoon cloves
Dash of pepper

Mix all the ingredients together. The dough will be very stiff and it may be necessary to use your hands to mix in the last of the flour. Roll the dough into "snakes" about ⅓ inch in diameter. Cut in ⅓-inch slices. Place the little cookies on a baking sheet. Bake at 350° for about 8 minutes.

Note: Putting the dough "snakes" in the freezer for a few minutes makes them easier to handle. Be sure to watch the baking cookies carefully. They are so small they burn easily.

Dansk Kringle
(Kringle Cookies)

3   cups flour
1   cup (16 tablespoons) butter or margarine
1   cup half and half
Pinch of salt
1   teaspoon baking powder
2   teaspoons sugar
2   teaspoons vanilla
1-2 tablespoons sugar for dipping

Mix all ingredients as for a piecrust. Roll the dough into thin "snakes" about ¼ inch thick. Cut into strips about 4 inches long. Shape each strip into a figure 8. Dip the top side of the cookie into the sugar. Place on a sprayed cookie sheet. Bake at 375° until lightly browned. Be sure the cookie sheets cool between each batch.

Note: Almond flavoring can be substituted for the vanilla.

Make kringles out of leftover pie dough. Just shape in a figure 8 and dip in sugar before baking. Tasty!

Danish Flags for the Christmas Tree

This is a typical Danish decoration, but the idea can be used for any nationality.

Red construction paper
White "correction fluid" pen
White ribbon, about ¼-inch wide
Glue or paste

Trace and cut out a pattern for the Danish flag. Fold the red paper. Place the pattern on the fold. Cut out a supply of the flags. Using the white "correction fluid" pen, color in the bars of the flag. Be sure to do this on both sides of the fold. Place the white ribbon in the fold of the flags. (Space the flags about 2" apart.) Glue the two sides of the flags together.

Note: Strips of white paper cut about ⅜-inch wide can be glued on the flags for the stripes instead of coloring them in.

A variation of this is to alternate Danish and American flags on the ribbon. Use purchased miniature American flags pasted together along with the Danish flags.

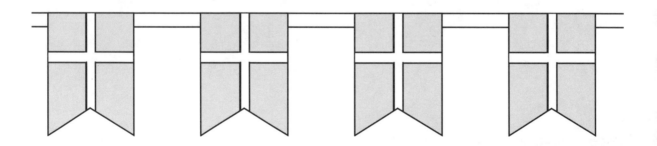

Driftwood from the Sea—
The Swedes in Texas

The day Poppa brought home the bundle, little Anna and her brothers and sisters knew Christmas was on its way. Carefully unwrapping the newspaper and twine, Momma unveiled several slabs of what the children thought looked like heavy pieces of dried driftwood. This was the special Christmas delicacy of *lutfisk*, an important Swedish tradition the family continued even after moving to Texas. When it arrived, Momma would work with it for several weeks to get it ready for the holiday.

First she would put it in a large tub of water to soak for about four days, changing the water every day. After draining and scrubbing the fish, she would cover it with slaked lime. She would then dissolve washing soda in warm water, cool it, and then pour the water over the fish. The fish needed to soak in this mixture for about a week. When the fish became soft, Momma would once again wash it thoroughly and rinse it with fresh water.

She had to scrub the tub again before the fish could be put back in it to soak another four or five days. To keep the water clear, she had to change it every day. If time were running out, she could let it stand under running water (as in a clear stream because there were no faucets as we have today!) for several hours a day for a couple of days. The fish was then ready to cook for Christmas dinner. Anna always watched and helped her mother, learning her methods for when she grew up and would prepare *lutfisk* for her family.

Today Anna, and any other Swedish descendant who wants to prepare this traditional Christmas Eve delicacy, buys the fish ready for cooking. This fluffy, white fish now comes ready to be dropped into boiling water or baked in the oven. The weeks and hours of work preparing it for cooking have, fortunately, been eliminated. Few people today have the time or desire to do all the work the early Swedish women did for their special Christmas Eve dinner.

Before the Civil War, only a handful of scattered Swedes had made it to Texas. Most of the Scandinavians who traveled across the Atlantic Ocean to the United States settled in the northern and midwestern states. But when Swen Magnus Swenson (Swenson means "Son of Swen"; Swen's father's first name was therefore also Swen) immigrated to the Houston area and made his fortune, he wanted other Swedes to succeed also. One of the first people he convinced to join him in Texas was his uncle, Swante Palm. They immediately became successful business partners. Together they became an informal, two-man recruiting and immigration service. They paid travel expenses for individuals and families to come to Texas on credit or in return for indentured service. Swenson also became a land agent who sold land to the Swedish newcomers. Within a few years the immigrants who worked hard found themselves more prosperous than they had dared dream before they came.

The first Swedish settlements were rural communities in the Austin area. Names such as New Sweden, Govalle (translates to "good grazing," which it was), Palm Valley, and Swensondale reflect their heritage and their benefactors. Like other groups of immigrants, they formed mutual aid societies to protect their members from fire, theft, and death. These organizations were based on the models of

the cooperatives they had experienced in Sweden. In the 1870s the Swedes in Decker, which is east of Austin, created an insurance society to record brands used on livestock. They also prosecuted horse thieves, a serious problem at the time, and reimbursed any member whose horse was stolen.

Letters by Swedish immigrants to relatives still in Sweden give us a glimpse into the reactions of the newcomers to their strange new world in Texas. One of Swante Palm's comments was, "The chief characteristic of weather in Texas is not variety, but surprise." Those of us who live in Texas today still agree with this statement about our weather. We are aware that it can be hot one day and forty degrees cooler the next after a "norther" has blown in. These vast fluctuations came as a surprise to these settlers who came from the more stable climes of northern Europe.

Fred Bergman, in a letter to his sister in Sweden, accurately summarized the immigrant experience: "Texas is a place for the poor to work their way up by means of work and thrift. Poor Swedes come here practically all the time, and in a few years they are independent. This place is not for a lazy bones."

The Christmas celebration for the Swedes begins on December 13, which is Saint Lucia's Day. Lucia was an Italian girl who gave her dowry to a poor family the night before her own wedding in the fourth century. Ultimately, she was accused of witchcraft and burned at the stake. Years later she appeared in Sweden during a famine to feed the people. To honor her, the oldest daughter rises early in the morning to serve coffee and buns to the parents. On her head she wears a wreath of greenery with seven lighted candles. Some Swedish families in Texas continued the tradition of the oldest daughter serving the parents breakfast in bed for St. Lucia's Day, but they very quickly eliminated the lighted candles. The risk of the daughter awakening her parents with screams from flaming hair was too great to continue that part of the tradition! Today the St. Lucia crown usually has battery-operated candles.

The Scandinavians during pagan times burned a huge log to honor Thor. The log was called the *juul*, which later became yule. The burning of the yule log between Christmas and New Year spread to England, Germany, and other Christian countries before it was brought to the United States.

It was Swen Swenson who brought to Texas the legend of a magic gift-giver who traveled about in a sleigh drawn by reindeer. *Jule-Nissen* was an elf who lived in the attic or hayloft of the family home. Only the family cat could see him. He was known for taking care of neglected animals as well as bringing gifts to children. On Christmas Eve the children would leave a bowl of rice porridge (rice pudding) for him. In many homes the father would dress in a red suit like *Jule-Nissen* to distribute gifts to the children on Christmas Eve. Sometimes he would throw the gifts into the house through an open window or door.

Santa Claus has replaced *Jule-Nissen* in Swedish homes today. Most of the descendants of the original settlers have assimilated into the melting pot of our state. The last Swedish-language newspaper in Texas quit publishing in the 1980s. However, ties with Sweden have continued to be strong. In 1988 the Swedes in Texas commemorated the 150th anniversary of the arrival of Swedes in Texas. King Carl XVI and Queen Silvia of Sweden attended the celebration.

After World War I, immigration to Texas from Sweden virtually stopped. Only in recent years with the advent of international companies operating in Texas have Swedes resumed moving here. But many of the Swedish traditions and foods continue to live on.

Swedish Recipes

Spenatsoppa
(Cream of Spinach Soup)

1 package (16 oz.) frozen chopped spinach

4 tablespoons butter or margarine

4 tablespoons flour

2 cups milk

2 cups chicken broth (or one can plus enough water to make 2 cups)

½ teaspoon salt

Dash of pepper

6 poached eggs (optional)

OR

6 hard-boiled eggs, chopped (optional)

Defrost and heat spinach in the microwave. Do not add water. On the stove, melt butter, add flour, and cook until it bubbles. Stir in milk and broth. Stir constantly over medium heat until soup thickens. Reduce heat to very low and cook for 10 minutes more. Stir in salt, pepper, and hot cooked spinach. Pour into soup bowls. Garnish with a poached egg, if desired, or sprinkle with chopped hard-boiled eggs.

Note: This recipe can be made with kale, chard, or almost any type of greens. A dash of cinnamon or the juice of one lemon gives this soup an interesting touch.

Mandelklimp
(Almond Dumplings)

2	tablespoons butter or margarine
1/3	cup milk
1/3	cup flour
1	teaspoon sugar
1/8	teaspoon salt
1	egg
1/4	teaspoon almond extract

Place butter and milk in a saucepan. Heat until milk is scalded and butter is melted. Add flour, salt, and sugar. Stir constantly until mixture forms a ball and leaves the side of the pan. Remove from heat. Add egg and almond extract and beat until smooth. Drop from teaspoon into gently boiling water or soup. Cook uncovered for 10 minutes. Cover and cook 10 minutes longer.

Note: This recipe makes about 30 small dumplings.

Try them in the cream of spinach soup (page 172).

Ugnsomelett
(Baked Omelet)

4	eggs
1½	teaspoons flour
1/8	teaspoon salt
1/8	teaspoon pepper
2	cups milk
1	tablespoon butter or margarine

Beat the eggs 1 minute. Beat in the flour, salt, pepper, and milk. Melt the butter in a 10-inch skillet or baking pan. Pour in the egg mixture. Bake at 350° for 25-30 minutes. Loosen the omelet with a spatula and turn over onto a large, warm serving platter.

Note: This omelet can be filled with whatever you like—cheese, mushrooms, picante sauce, jelly, or anything else. The Swedes liked to fill theirs with creamed vegetables or fish. When you make the spinach soup on page 172, reduce the milk in half to make creamed spinach. It is great on this omelet. Or you can eat it without any filling if you prefer.

Oven Pancake

1 cup flour
1½ teaspoons sugar
¼ teaspoon salt
2 eggs
2 cups milk
¼ pound ham

Mix the flour, sugar, and salt. Beat the eggs until light, add the milk, and beat again until well mixed. Add the egg mixture to the flour mixture and beat until smooth. Let the batter stand for 1 hour. Cut the ham into small cubes. Grease or spray a 10-inch frying pan or similar ovenproof pan. Stir the batter and pour it into the pan. Sprinkle ham over the top. Bake at 450° for 20-25 minutes.

Stekta Tomater
(Browned Tomato Halves)

This is a quick, easy side dish that adds a touch of elegance to an ordinary meal.

3 tomatoes
3 tablespoons flour
¼ teaspoon salt
2 tablespoons butter

Cut a thin slice off each end of the tomatoes. Then cut tomatoes in half. Mix flour and salt. Dip the tomatoes in the flour. Melt the butter in a frying pan. Add tomatoes and fry until lightly brown on both sides.

Note: Don't overcook the tomatoes or they will be mushy.

Fiskbullar
(Fish Balls)

This is a great recipe for using leftover fish and mashed potatoes. In fact, dry, day-old mashed potatoes work best!

1½ cups cooked fish

1   cup mashed potatoes

1   egg, beaten

½ teaspoon white pepper

1   teaspoon salt

3   tablespoons flour

1   egg, slightly beaten

½ cup bread or cracker crumbs

Oil, butter, or margarine for frying

Mash the fish until it is crumbly. Add mashed potatoes, one beaten egg, pepper, and salt. Mix lightly with fork. Form into 1½-inch balls. Roll the balls in the flour, then in a beaten egg, then in the crumbs. Let rest for a half hour. Fry until lightly browned, about 7 minutes. Drain. Serve hot or cold.

Note: Any type of cooked fish can be used in this recipe, but white fish works best. If the mashed potatoes are creamy and moist, a little extra flour and crumbs may be needed.

These fish balls are delicious either hot or cold. Serve with homemade mushroom or fish sauce, or your favorite bottled cocktail or remoulade sauce. I personally like the Ukrainian dill sauce (page 88) with these. Try it!

Ugnstekt Lutfisk
(Baked Lutfisk)

Buy the lutfisk ready to cook at a specialty market. This is so much easier than preparing the dried fish like grandmother used to do!

3   pounds prepared lutfisk (ready to cook)

Cut prepared lutfisk into serving pieces. Rinse and drain well. Place skin side down in a large, shallow baking pan that has been lightly sprayed with a nonstick cooking spray. Bake at 325° for 35 minutes.

Note: Lutfisk is traditionally served with cream sauce. To make it authentic, use fish broth in your favorite cream sauce recipe.

Kottbulla
(Meatballs)

These are nothing like the cocktail meatballs swimming in barbecue sauce that sometimes masquerade as Swedish meatballs. These are so much better!

½   cup fine dry bread crumbs
⅔   cup milk
1   egg
2   tablespoons minced onion
1   teaspoon salt
⅛   teaspoon pepper
⅛   teaspoon nutmeg
1   pound ground beef
2   tablespoons butter or margarine
¼   cup water

Mix bread crumbs and milk. Beat in egg and onion. Add salt, pepper, nutmeg, and ground beef. Mix thoroughly. Divide meat mixture into 50-60 even portions. Shape into small balls. Melt butter in a skillet. Brown meatballs thoroughly, shaking pan occasionally to keep the balls round. Add water and cover the skillet. Simmer about 20 minutes until done. Add more water, if needed.

Kalops
(Browned Beef Stew)

2 tablespoons shortening or oil
2 pounds stew beef, cut in 2-inch cubes
2 onions, sliced
3 cups water
½ teaspoon salt
3 bay leaves (laurel)
2 teaspoons whole allspice
2 tablespoons cornstarch
½ cup cold water

Brown the beef cubes and onion slices in the shortening. Add the water and the seasonings. Cover and simmer 2-2½ hours until the meat is tender. Mix the cornstarch with the cold water. Stir it into the meat mixture, stirring until the broth is thickened. Simmer an additional 10 minutes, uncovered.

Note: Serve with boiled potatoes or rice for a hearty supper.

Spetskako
(Lace Cookies)

2 cups firmly packed dark brown sugar
1 cup melted butter
1 egg
2 cups oatmeal (not instant)
1 teaspoon vanilla
Pinch of salt

Mix sugar and melted butter. Stir in egg. Add oatmeal and vanilla. Mix well. Drop ½ teaspoonfuls of batter on an ungreased cookie sheet, about 2 inches apart. Bake at 350° for 7 minutes. Remove from oven and cool for a few minutes.

Hold the cookie sheet over a warm burner and remove cookies with a spatula. Cookies will be paper thin, lacy looking, and very crisp.

Note: It takes a little practice to learn how to remove the cookies from the cookie sheet. If they do not come off neatly, reshape while still warm and let them cool on wax paper. Crumbled cookies make an excellent topping for ice cream, puddings, and cobblers.

Nötkakor
(Nut Cookies)

2   cups flour

¼   teaspoon salt

6   tablespoons sugar

1   cup butter or margarine (16 table-
    spoons) at room temperature

1   cup ground pecans

1   teaspoon vanilla

Sugar, candied cherries, or pecan halves

Mix the flour, salt, and sugar on a clean surface. Add the butter, nuts, and vanilla.

Mix into a smooth dough using your hands. Shape into rolls about 1½ inches in diameter. Wrap in plastic wrap. Chill in the refrigerator several hours or overnight. Slice very thin. Arrange on a sprayed cookie sheet. Sprinkle with sugar or decorate with a piece of cherry or a pecan half. Bake at 375° for 8-10 minutes.

Spritz

1   cup butter or margarine (16 table-
    spoons)

¾   cup sugar

1   egg

1   teaspoon almond extract

2½ cups flour

½   teaspoon double-acting baking powder

Pinch of salt

Sugar, if desired

Cream the butter. Add the sugar and cream again. Beat in the egg and almond extract. Mix together the flour, baking powder, and salt. Add to the butter mixture and mix well. Put the dough in a cookie press using a disk with a small star opening. Press the dough into an "S" or "O" shape on an ungreased cookie sheet. Bake at 400° for 10-12 minutes. If desired, sprinkle with sugar before baking.

Note: Colored sugar looks really festive on these cookies.

Deg For Kaffebrod
(Sweet Coffee Bread)

This is a very versatile dough. Use it to make Lucia buns or Swedish tea rings. Whatever you make with it, it will be delicious and you will receive raves from everyone who tastes it.

2	packages rapid rise yeast
⅔	cup sugar
5	cups flour
¾	cup scalded milk, cooled to lukewarm
½	cup lukewarm water
½	cup soft butter or margarine
2	eggs
1	teaspoon salt
1	teaspoon powdered cardamom seed

Mix 2 cups of flour with the yeast and other dry ingredients. Add the liquids and beat until smooth. Add the butter and eggs and mix well. Add the remaining flour. Knead the dough on a floured surface until it is smooth and elastic. (Or use your food processor with the kneading blade.) Let rest for 10 minutes. Shape into Lucia buns or tea rings. Let rise until double in size. Bake according to the directions for each shape.

Tekransa
(Tea Rings)

A beautiful Swedish tea ring always elicits "ooo's" and "ahh's" from your guests. It looks too good to eat but tastes even better!

Dough for Sweet Coffee Bread

- ¼ cup melted butter
- ½ cup sugar
- 2 teaspoons cinnamon
- ½ cup chopped nuts (almonds, pecans, walnuts, or other nuts)
- 1 egg white, slightly beaten
- 1 tablespoon cold water
- 2 tablespoons sugar

Divide the Sweet Coffee Bread dough into 2 pieces. On a lightly floured surface, roll one piece into a rectangle about 10 x 16 inches. Brush with 2 tablespoons melted butter. Sprinkle with ¼ cup sugar, 1 teaspoon cinnamon, and ¼ cup chopped nuts. Roll up like a jellyroll. Place on a cookie sheet and form into a ring. Using scissors, cut most of the way through the ring at ½-inch intervals. Turn each slice on its side to the outside of the ring. Let rise until doubled. Mix egg white and water. Brush the egg mixture over the dough. Sprinkle with 1 tablespoon sugar. Bake at 350° for 30 to 35 minutes.

Repeat with the other half of the pastry.

Note: To make this tea ring even more festive, drizzle with powdered sugar icing. Decorate with additional chopped nuts, maraschino cherries, or a few bits of candied fruit.

Lussekattor
(Lucia Buns)

These buns are a special treat at Christmas or any time of the year!

Dough for Sweet Coffee Bread
¼   cup seedless raisins
1   egg white, slightly beaten
1   tablespoon cold water

Cut the dough into 32 pieces. Roll each piece until it is about 16 inches long. Cut each strip in half. Place the two 8-inch strips side by side. Curl out each of the four ends to shape the bun. Put a raisin in each curved end. Let rise until double in bulk, about half an hour. Mix the egg white with water and brush each bun. Bake at 350° for 11 to 12 minutes.

Note: Drizzle with powdered sugar icing, if desired, to further gild the lily.

Kryddkaka
(Spice Cake)

2   eggs
1   cup sugar
1   cup sour cream
1   tablespoon dark corn syrup
1   tablespoon melted butter or margarine
2   cups flour
1   teaspoon baking soda
1   teaspoon ground cloves
½   teaspoon cinnamon

Beat eggs. Add sugar, sour cream, syrup, and melted butter. Mix well. Add the dry ingredients and mix gently. Pour the batter into a greased and floured or sprayed tube or bundt pan. Bake at 350° for 50-60 minutes. Dust with powdered sugar, if desired.

Adjustments to a New Land—
The Syrian-Lebanese in Texas

At the Saturday night dance in Longview, Texas, the parents, aunts, and uncles watched the teenagers dance. They spoke approvingly to one another in Arabic when one of their own danced with another son or daughter of Lebanese parents. The introduction of the young people to other Lebanese was the purpose of driving from Marshall or Waco or one of the other areas where Lebanese families had settled when they immigrated to Texas around the turn of the century. The hope was always that matches would be made that would eventually lead to marriage. If the older generation could no longer arrange marriages as in the past, they could do the next best thing: arrange for dances and other social occasions where the young people could meet others of Lebanese descent.

If the effort proved successful and a marriage resulted, all the Lebanese came to the wedding. Not only was it a celebration, but it was also another social occasion where the young could interact and then maybe there would be another wedding later—and another chance to make more matches. Whenever a Lebanese got married, even to an "outsider," the event was a huge affair attended by all the friends and relatives. Many traveled from a great distance to attend the festivities. The guests celebrated the entire weekend, even if the bride and groom left shortly after the ceremony.

Though they spoke Arabic, immigrants from Syria and Lebanon were Christian rather than Moslems. In fact, the discrimination against Christians was one of the reasons so many left during the late nineteenth and early twentieth centuries. Most belonged to the Eastern Orthodox Church and followed that service for weddings. The long, elaborate ceremony included the burning of incense and chanting by the priest. During a traditional dance performed around the altar, the bride and groom were crowned king and queen of the new home they created with their marriage. The Eastern Orthodox ceremony today is very much like it was then. After the church ceremony, the couple and all the guests then went to someone's home or the church hall for a feast that included traditional foods such as *kibbee* and *tahini* served alongside favorite American dishes. The dancing and singing continued late into the night.

The most important ingredients at any celebration were family, food, and music. For every event from a baptism to a marriage to a funeral, the extended family always gathered. No need existed for formal invitations because everyone knew they were welcome, even those friends and relatives from other towns. Everyone who was able helped prepare the food. Each woman brought her specialty, thus ensuring a large variety of tasty treats. In later years as wealth increased, the celebrations grew even larger and even more elaborate. They became huge, catered events held in hotels, but the most important ingredients—family, food, and music—remained the same.

At every gathering, stories were told in the oral tradition of minstrels. Songs passed down for generations told stories of the past in the old country. Other tales might even have been made up on the spot to describe the event that was taking place. They may have been told in song, with the melody and words being devised as the

singer performed. Dancing the traditional *dabke* and other folk dances to the mystical, wailing music of lutes, hand drums, and tambourines further kept the memories of their heritage alive. But then the young people always managed to dance some of the new popular American dances, too.

Until Lebanon became a separate nation in 1919, the province of the Ottoman Empire that included Greater Syria and Mount Lebanon was known as Syria. The passports of those from Mount Lebanon identified them as Syrian-Lebanese. Until World War I, when restrictions were placed on immigration, many came from this area to the United States and especially to Texas. Like other immigrants at this time, they left because of economic hardships, overpopulation, and religious and social discrimination.

In Texas they became citizens of the United States, and many distinguished themselves in the armed services. On the dog tags that all military personnel wear for identification, the designation for people who practiced the Eastern Orthodox religion was originally "O." Unfortunately, this confused medics who interpreted it as blood type, sometimes with disastrous results. The abbreviation was changed to "EO" to eliminate this confusion. And hopefully to save lives!

If the number of Lebanese in an area was not large enough to support their own church, they often became part of

another group such as the Episcopalians, but they still maintained their unique Lebanese traditions.

Typically, one member of a family would come to the United States, get a job, and work to save money to bring the other relatives here. Galveston and Indianola were the favorite ports of entry into Texas. In 1856 over thirty camels were brought to Indianola from Syria-Lebanon to see if they could be used as beasts of burden and for transportation. Although this experiment was interrupted by the destruction of Indianola by a hurricane, it did represent a part of the Lebanese heritage.

Regardless of which port of entry the newcomer came through, the final destination was always the town where the relatives resided. Once someone arrived, the Lebanese community greeted him with a warm, enthusiastic welcome—and often a job.

Like the other groups that immigrated to Texas, the Lebanese came to seek their fortune. But unlike the other groups, they did not come to Texas to become farmers and landowners. They participated in commerce rather than agriculture, so they settled in towns and cities where there was already a population that could support their stores and shops.

The earliest immigrants in the late eighteen hundreds frequently began as itinerant peddlers with a *keskey*, or pack, and later a wagon filled with goods to sell to the people in small, isolated communities and towns. They sold notions, laces, potions, and religious items from the Holy Land. Eventually they became merchants wherever they settled. Later generations diversified into other professional fields, as well as continuing in all aspects of merchandising and manufacturing.

New arrivals to Texas would live with the sponsoring relative until they could afford their own homes. The result was a network of extended families throughout the area that gathered frequently for dances and other celebrations so the young people could gather, meet each other, and hopefully marry.

The new families lived in homes near the relatives, thereby forming close-knit Lebanese enclaves that continued to follow many of the old traditions. Often feeling like outsiders from the mainstream society in the towns where they settled, such as Waco, Beaumont, San Antonio, and elsewhere, they isolated themselves. This further reinforced the continuation of their ethnic traditions.

On Christmas Eve all the relatives would call on the patriarch of the community to pay their respects. At his home, each visitor would imbibe a glass of wine and some food before venturing to the next household. Visiting ten or more homes on Christmas Eve and eating and drinking at each one was not at all unusual. Since all this eating and drinking occurred over a long period of time, drunkenness and overeating were very rare.

January 6, the day of the Epiphany, is also a day of remembering. It is a time to remember that Christmas does not end on the evening of December 25. Instead it was a time to remember that this is the day of Christmas celebrations in Lebanon. It was a day to remember the life they had left behind, as well as the family members and friends still there. Family ties were very important to the Lebanese who came to Texas in the late nineteenth and early twentieth centuries. This remains the same today.

However, they did incorporate American ways into their lives. Public schools provided for the education of their children. In the process of educating the children, they assimilated into the mainstream of American life. Many went on to college and then on to careers in all parts of the state and country. Yet there is still a tendency for people of Lebanese descent to live in close proximity to one another.

Few of the immigrants taught their native Arabic to their children. Don Barkett, who grew up in Marshall, Texas, remembers asking his immigrant father to teach him his language. His father replied by telling him that as an American, he would never need to speak Arabic. Fortunately, just by listening to the older generation speaking Arabic, he did manage to pick up a few words and phrases. Like many other Texans, Don spent his career in the oil industry. While working for Dow Chemical he frequently traveled to Lebanon as well as other Arabic-speaking countries. With his Lebanese roots he found an instant rapport with his business associates. The original form of his last name was "Barrakkatt" which means "blessings." A common expression in Lebanon is to bestow blessings on another by saying the word "barrakkatt." During his time there, Mr. Barkett frequently assumed the salutation was someone calling his name! His heritage became a link to his future.

Syrian-Lebanese Recipes

T'ai bien—This is good!
A comment frequently heard at Lebanese meals.

Tahini is a basic ingredient in many Lebanese recipes. It is a thick sesame seed paste. Usually there is a layer of oil on the top that must be mixed in before using. The original Lebanese settlers in Texas would make their own; however, now it is available in most large supermarkets.

Taratoor
(Basic Tahini Sauce)

1 cup *tahini*
3 large garlic cloves
½ cup lemon juice (or more to taste)
½ teaspoon salt
½-¾ cup water

Blend the *tahini*, garlic, and salt in a blender or food processor. Add the lemon juice while continuing to blend. Slowly add water until it reaches a mayonnaise consistency. Store in the refrigerator.

Note: Serve with crackers, fresh vegetables, or cooked meats. This also is great basted on fish during the last few minutes of baking.

Hoomus B'Tahini
(Chickpea Dip)

2   cans (15 oz.) chickpeas (garbanzos)

5   large cloves garlic, crushed

4½ tablespoons *tahini*

1   tablespoon olive oil

1   teaspoon salt

Juice of 2 lemons

4   tablespoons water

Toasted sesame seeds or sprigs of mint
(optional)

Boil chickpeas in the liquid from the can for 5 minutes. Drain the beans in a colander and let cool. Remove the hulls. Add the other ingredients and blend until smooth in a blender or food processor. Garnish with toasted sesame seeds or sprigs of mint, if desired.

Note: Serve at room temperature with pita bread.

If this is too much garlic for you, reduce the amount. You can always add more!

Pita Chips

This is a quick, easy chip to serve with any dip or to eat just plain.

Cut each pita into 8 wedges. Separate the 2 layers of each wedge. Place on a sprayed baking sheet. Bake at 350° until brown, about 10 minutes.

Yogurt and Cucumber Soup

This is a cool, refreshing soup for hot Texas summers.

1   large cucumber
2½ cups plain yogurt
1   clove garlic, crushed
1   teaspoon dried mint or 1 tablespoon fresh mint

Wash the cucumber, but do not peel it. Coarsely chop the cucumber. Sprinkle it with salt and allow it to stand for about 30 minutes. Drain and rinse the cucumber. Put all the ingredients into a blender or food processor. Blend until the soup is creamy. Chill and serve in chilled bowls.

Note: If desired, garnish with diced fresh tomatoes and a sprig of dill.

Tomato Salad

2   or more chopped tomatoes
2   tablespoons onion, grated or finely chopped
2   tablespoons fresh mint or 1 tablespoon dried mint
1   tablespoon olive oil
Juice of ½ lemon
Dash of pepper
Dash of salt (optional)

Chill the tomatoes. Mix the remaining ingredients to make a dressing for the tomatoes. Add the dressing to the tomatoes. Stir lightly. Cover and chill for at least another 15 minutes. Right before serving, stir one more time.

Note: Small cubes of mozzarella or goat cheese are delicious in this.

Unstuffed Squash

Stuffed yellow squash (Mishee-Koosa) is a favorite Lebanese dish. Unstuffed squash is very similar, except it is made as a casserole to eliminate the necessity of coring the squash.

1 cup uncooked rice
½ pound ground beef or lamb
4 cups sliced yellow squash
1 can (15 oz.) stewed tomatoes
2 tablespoons oil
1 medium onion, chopped
½ teaspoon cinnamon (or more, to taste)
Salt and pepper to taste

Sauté the onion in the oil. Add tomatoes and seasonings. Simmer then remove from heat. Mix rice and ground meat, being sure all the pieces are small.

Add the rice mixture to the tomatoes and onions. Alternate layers of squash and rice-meat mixture in a large pot. Add enough water to cover the mixture by about an inch. Cover. Slow boil about 30 minutes until the rice and squash are tender. Add more water, if needed. DO NOT STIR! Occasionally run a table knife around the sides and in the middle of the pot to distribute the liquid.

Note: The remaining liquid makes a delicious broth that is served like gravy.

Spinach with Wheat

¼ cup cracked wheat (bulgur)
1 pound fresh or frozen spinach, chopped
1 onion, chopped
¼ cup oil
½ teaspoon cinnamon
Salt and pepper to taste

Soak the bulgur in 2 cups of water for 15 minutes or until the water is soaked in. Sauté onion in oil until it is clear. Add spinach. (Frozen spinach should be thawed and well squeezed.) Season and cook until spinach is tender. Add wheat. Heat for an additional 15 minutes.

Chickpea Croquettes

Easy and tasty!

1   can (15 oz.) chickpeas (garbanzos)
1   medium potato, boiled and mashed
1½ cups fresh parsley, chopped
2   tablespoons olive oil
½   teaspoon garlic salt
¾   cup flour

Drain and rinse the chickpeas. Pulverize them in a food processor. Add the remaining ingredients except flour. Mix well.

Shape into small balls. Roll in the flour to coat. Fry in oil. Serve cold.

Note: Stuff several croquettes into a pita half, along with shredded lettuce and chopped tomatoes and cucumbers. Top with plain yogurt, *Hoomus B'Tahini*, or ranch dressing for a tasty but different sandwich. These can also be used instead of croutons to give a salad a Middle Eastern touch.

Lemon Chicken

This is a great dish to serve to company because there is so little last-minute work.

3-4 pounds raw chicken, cubed
2   large onions, chopped
3   large cloves garlic, crushed
¾   cup lemon juice
Salt and pepper to taste
3-4 tablespoons butter

Mix onions, garlic, lemon juice, salt, and pepper. Pour over chicken. Cover and marinate in refrigerator overnight. Sauté the chicken in the butter. Add the marinade and more lemon juice and water if more liquid is needed. Cover and simmer over low heat until tender, about 30 minutes.

Note: This is delicious served over Nutty Rice (page 192) or plain white or brown rice. Garnish with toasted pine nuts or mint leaves, if desired.

Snobar Ib Rooz
(Nutty Rice)

2   cans (10½ oz.) chicken broth

1   cup rice

1   stick (8 tablespoons) butter or margarine

½   cup pine nuts (*snobar*)

½   teaspoon salt

1   tablespoon instant minced onion

½   teaspoon cinnamon

¼   teaspoon pepper

Sauté the pine nuts in the butter. Add rice, onion, and seasonings. Stir in chicken broth. Cover. Bake at 350° for 1 hour. Add extra water if needed.

Nutty Rice and Chicken Casserole

Nutty Rice

4   skinless chicken breasts

Follow the instructions for making Nutty Rice, above. Place the chicken breasts on top of the rice after adding the chicken broth. Cover and bake at 350° for 1 hour.

Ruz Shrriyeh
(Vermicelli)

½ cup butter
1 cup vermicelli
¼ cup pine nuts
1 chicken bouillon cube
½ teaspoon cinnamon
¼ teaspoon white pepper
Dash of cayenne
1 cup rice
3 cups water

Sauté the vermicelli in butter until golden. Add the pine nuts. Stir until brown. Remove from heat and stir in rice, coating well. Add the bouillon cube and spices. Add water and bring to a boil. Simmer for 30 minutes. Serve hot.

Easy Basic Bread Dough

2 cups self-rising flour
½ cup milk
¼ cup oil

Scald the milk and then let it cool to lukewarm. Mix all the ingredients. Knead the dough until it is smooth and elastic. Form into a ball and place in a greased bowl, being sure to have oil on all sides. Let rest until light and springy, about an hour. Divide dough into 2 balls. Roll each ball into a 6-8 inch circle that is about ½ inch thick. Let the loaves rest for about 10-15 minutes. Bake on an ungreased baking sheet for 12-15 minutes at 450° until golden brown.

Note: This dough can also be used in any recipe requiring dough such as meat or spinach pies.

Kibbee
(Ground Meat)

Kibbee is a traditional dish that is always served at any type of holiday or celebration. It is also an everyday food. It is usually made with ground lamb, although ground beef is sometimes used. Sometimes it was served raw, similar to tartar. However, today it is recommended that all ground meats be thoroughly cooked.

1¼ cups cracked wheat (bulgur)
1   pound finely ground lean lamb
2   large onions, finely grated
½   tablespoon salt
½   teaspoon black pepper
¼   teaspoon red pepper
¼   teaspoon cinnamon

Soak the cracked wheat in 3 cups of water for 30 minutes. With wet hands, mix all the ingredients together by kneading as for bread until well mixed. The raw *kibbee* will look like meatloaf. Use the *kibbee* in another recipe or cook in patties like hamburgers.

Note: Be sure to keep your hands wet when you mix the lamb and wheat mixture. *Kibbee* can be used in miniature meat pies or *kibbee* soup. Cooked *kibbee* can also be used as a filling in pita with lettuce, tomatoes, and cucumbers, garnished with *tahini* sauce or with plain yogurt.

Miniature Meat Pies

1   can regular refrigerator biscuits or Easy Basic Bread Dough

½   recipe of *kibbee*

OR

½   pound ground lamb

½   small onion, finely chopped

4   teaspoons olive oil

1   tablespoon fresh mint or ½ tablespoon dried mint

¼   cup toasted pine nuts

⅛   teaspoon salt

⅛   teaspoon pepper

⅛   teaspoon cinnamon

⅛   teaspoon cayenne

Prepare *kibbee* or sauté onions in olive oil until clear. Add lamb and brown. Add the remaining ingredients. Simmer for 5 minutes.

Cut each biscuit in half. Flatten each half with oiled hands and put on a baking sheet. Press lamb mixture or kibbee into each biscuit half. Bake at 325° until brown. Serve hot.

Note: These miniature meat pies make a great but easy hot appetizer or hearty snack. Serve with minced mint, *tahini* sauce, or a little plain yogurt.

Kibbee Soup

1   can (10½ oz.) condensed chicken broth

3   cans water

¼   recipe of raw *kibbee*

½   cup rice

¼   teaspoon cinnamon

½   teaspoon salt

½   teaspoon pepper

Roll the *kibbee* into small balls. Heat the broth and water. Add the *kibbee* balls to the liquid. Cook until almost done, about 20 minutes. Add rice and seasonings and simmer until the rice is done.

Note: Chopped red or green peppers, zucchini, or yellow squash can be added to give the soup color and a slightly different flavor.

Salata Dressing
(Salad Dressing)

½ cup fresh lemon juice

½ cup olive oil

2 tablespoons fresh mint, chopped

2 cloves garlic, crushed

Salt and pepper to taste

Place all the ingredients in a jar with a tight-fitting lid. Shake well. Refrigerate.

Note: This can be used as a salad dressing, meat marinade, or sauce for vegetables.

Shish Kabobs

1 pound lamb, cubed

1 cup Salata Dressing

1 red or green pepper

1 onion

1 zucchini or yellow squash

2 firm tomatoes (Roma tomatoes or similar)

Marinate the lamb overnight in Salata Dressing. Cut the vegetables in chunks large enough to skewer. Alternate the meat and vegetables on the skewers. Brush the vegetables with the marinade. Broil or grill until done.

Note: This is delicious served over plain rice or Nutty Rice (page 192). Additional Salata Dressing can be served on the side. Do not reuse leftover marinade.

Almond Fingers

12 sheets phyllo pastry
¾ cup melted butter or margarine
⅓ cup sugar
1 cup finely ground almonds
¼ teaspoon cinnamon
Powdered sugar

Combine the almonds, sugar, and cinnamon. Cut each pastry sheet into 3 rectangles and brush each with melted butter. Put a heaping teaspoonful of almond mixture in the center of each rectangle. Fold in the sides and roll into a "finger." Place fingers on a greased baking sheet. Bake at 350° for 30 minutes or until pastry is golden. Remove immediately to a cooling rack. Dust with powdered sugar.

Note: Grind the almonds in your food processor. Be sure to quickly brush each phyllo sheet with butter to prevent it from drying and becoming brittle. These are delicious and worth the work!

Beyond Pasta—
Italians in Texas

Spending Saturday afternoon at the mall is a typical teenage activity.

But this group of young people did not come to the mall to hang out with their friends or to shop. These young people are descendants of Italian settlers who came to Texas and are part of the Italian-American Club in Dallas. This group is at the mall to perform a play about the good witch La Befana. According to legend, she comes down the chimney on Epiphany Eve to bring gifts to good boys and girls. Once she has left, a bell chimes to tell the children that she has paid her annual visit. And then, of course, they wake up and come scrambling into the parlor to see what she has brought.

On other weekends these same teens may be performing traditional Italian dances at a folk festival somewhere in the state. Or they may be participating in a service project for underprivileged children or another worthy cause. Benevolence is an important tenant in the lives of Italian Texans. It may take the form of money donations, but just as likely it will be hands-on service that the charity-minded

Italians provide along with their children. It is no surprise then that the Salvation Army, an organization known for its good deeds towards the less fortunate, was brought to Texas by an Italian, Adam Janelli, an immigrant from Parma, Italy.

Prior to the great influx of immigrants that began in the second half of the nineteenth century, only a few individual Italians had made it to Texas. The first known Italian to see Texas was Amerigo Vespucci, the mapmaker who gave his name to our continent in the New World. Among the few Italians who were here during Texas War of Independence from Mexico, it is ironic that some fought for the Mexicans and others for the Texans!

Beginning in the 1880s, more Italians began arriving and settling in Texas, especially in Galveston, Houston, and San Antonio. Southern Italians who chose farming settled along the Brazos River near the towns of Bryan and Hearne. A few Northern Italians settled in Montague County near the Red River in North Texas. Like other ethnic groups that came to Texas at this time, the Italians left Europe because of economic depression and warfare. Many of the first to arrive during this wave of immigration were young men who came to seek their fortunes. Once they were able, they brought wives and families to their new homes. These young men provided labor for the coal mines of Thurber and the building of the railway between Victoria and Rosenberg. This railroad was promoted and built by the Italian Count Joseph Telfener and was nicknamed the "Macaroni Line" after the favorite food of so many of the workers. The town of Edna, which is now the county seat of Jackson County, was named after the count's daughter. Not far from Edna is another small town named Louise. A popular joke in this area suggested sleeping between Edna and Louise for the night! Of course, the joke referred to the towns.

When their labor was no longer needed for the mines or the railroads, the Italian laborers moved on, often settling in the same areas as their fellow Italian immigrants. Once they settled, a number of Italians rose to positions of prominence. Among these were Pompeo Coppini of San Antonio whose sculptures are displayed on the capitol grounds in Austin, and Josephine Lucchese who became an internationally known opera singer in the 1920s.

A barber from Sicily, Charles Saverio Papa, printed the first Italian language newspaper in Texas. He arrived in Dallas in 1908 and called it "Venice" because of the unusual floods that year. For over fifty years his *La Tribuna Italiana* supported Italian communities in three states. When Mussolini declared war against the Allies in 1940, the paper started publishing in English and changed its name to *The Texas Tribune*. The paper ceased publication in 1962 because it had fulfilled its original purpose—the assimilation of Italians into American society.

March 19 of each year is St. Joseph's Day. The people of the island of Sicily faced a time of drought and famine and were near starvation. They prayed to their patron saint St. Joseph to intercede on their behalf to provide good crops. In return, they promised to remember his goodness and every year honor him by feeding those less fortunate. When the rains came and the crops prospered, they remembered their pledge, and the community began the tradition of offering their most prized possessions—food. Today this tradition is continued in the celebration of St. Joseph's Altar.

The St. Joseph's Altar celebration is a time to give thanks for the answer to a prayer such as the healing or return of a loved one (as from illness or war) and to share with others the prosperity and good fortune that one has received. Some St. Joseph's Altar celebrations are huge, with thousands of people

attending. Instead of actually inviting and feeding the poor at the altar as was originally done, most groups enjoy the celebration, then make a generous contribution to a charity to help the needy.

Preparations are begun weeks in advance as a coordinated, communal effort of the Italian community. The days of each family having its own St. Joseph's Altar have passed. However, the celebration may be sponsored by an individual or by a group such as the local chapter of the Italian American Society. Each person or family gives or does what he or she can. Some may cook one of the delicacies and others may be involved in the decorations or coordination of the event. Today the St. Joseph's Altar is usually held at a church hall or hotel to accommodate all the people who attend. Regardless of where the celebration occurs, certain elements are essential.

A three-tiered altar represents the Trinity. Originally it was adorned with the best grains, fruits, and vegetables. Today ornately decorated breads, cakes, and cookies are on the altar. Many of these offerings are symbolic. For example, St. Joseph's bread is a large golden loaf often covered in sesame seeds. It is shaped into a wreath to represent the crown of thorns worn by Christ. A basket of dyed eggs foreshadows the coming of Easter. Fish represent Christ's feeding of the multitudes.

No meat is ever served on the St. Joseph's Altar because the celebration occurs during Lent. Instead, the main entree is always pasta. The tomato sauce is made with a fish stock base, anchovies, sardines, and pine nuts. Browned bread crumbs are sprinkled on top rather than cheese to represent the sawdust of St. Joseph the carpenter.

Before the time of the famine, the fava bean was used as feed for cattle. However, food became so scarce that the people had to cook them and eat the beans themselves. Today, the Italians still consider it lucky to have a fava bean in your pocket!

Another part of the St. Joseph's Altar celebration is the reenactment of the story of the Holy Family performed by children dressed in costumes. Special saints may also be represented in the performance. Afterwards, the "Holy Family" and "Saints" are the first to be served from the many foods on the altar. Only when they have finished may everyone else eat. Prayers and hymns accompany the meal. Even today the expression "May St. Joseph always smile upon you!" is used.

Christmas is another time of interesting Italian traditions. Christmas Eve is traditionally a day of fasting, although this custom is rarely observed today. The evening meal consists of seven different types of fish or seafood. The manner of preparation is not as important as having seven different varieties. These may include anchovies, sardines, mussels, clams, lobster, or any other variety that is available. Pasta will also be served as well as many special desserts. The meal is always served with the entire family seated around the table. Grown children will return to their parents' home with their families. Other relatives and friends are also included in the festivities. With all the different foods and people, the meal can easily take several hours. Then, after midnight, everyone opens gifts. Christmas Day is reserved for worship. After attending church services, the family joins together for another huge meal, this time containing meat.

The legend of La Befana began during the pre-Christian era. The Roman Befana was a sprite or fairy queen. She was incorporated into Christianity as a housewife too busy to go with the wise men to see the infant Jesus. When she changed her mind, she searched the world for them. When she could not find them, she roamed the earth on the eve of the Epiphany. Along the way she stopped to give gifts to good Italian children and lumps of coal to the bad ones. Her name comes from *epiphania,* or epiphany. A few families still give gifts on this day in addition to having Santa Claus on Christmas Eve.

La Befana, like the descendants of the Italian immigrants to Texas, is recognized for her giving. That is one tradition the Italian Texans still uphold.

Italian Recipes

Northern Italians make their sauces more tart than southern Italians. Those from southern Italy make theirs sweeter. To this day, the descendants of Italian immigrants still enjoy the traditional spaghetti and meatballs.

Pepperoni Pie

2   cups pepperoni, chopped
2   cups milk
2   eggs, beaten
1   cup mozzarella cheese, shredded
1½ cups flour

Mix all the ingredients together. Pour into a greased or sprayed 9 x 11-inch pan. Bake at 400° for 30 minutes, until knife inserted in center comes out clean. Serve cut into squares.

Note: This is great served as an appetizer or for brunch.

Basic Marinara Sauce

3-4 tablespoons olive oil
1   can (16 oz.) crushed tomatoes
¼   teaspoon oregano
1   clove garlic, minced
1   teaspoon dried basil

Sauté the garlic in the olive oil. Remove the pan from the heat and add the remaining ingredients. Simmer for 30 minutes, adding water as needed.

Variations:

Add one or more of the following to the basic recipe:

Sauté a small chopped onion with the garlic. Add ¼ cup white wine with the tomatoes. Add 1 tablespoon chopped fresh basil instead of dried. Add 1 tablespoon chopped fresh parsley. Add ¼ teaspoon fennel seed. Use a different variety of tomatoes—crushed plum tomatoes, for example. Serve with cooked meatballs. Use your imagination!

Vuccidrato
(St. Joseph's Bread)

1 cup sugar

1 teaspoon salt

2 packages rapid rise yeast

3 eggs

4 cups warm water

½ cup oil

10-15 cups flour

1 egg, beaten

In a large bowl, mix together the sugar, salt, yeast, and 6 cups flour. Heat the water and oil just until bubbles begin to appear. Stir the water into the dry ingredients. Add the eggs and mix well. Add enough flour to make a dough. Knead the dough on a floured board until smooth. If the dough is sticky, add more flour. Let the dough rest for 10 minutes. Divide the dough into thirds. Shape each piece into a long "snake." Braid the three "snakes." Bring the ends together to form a ring. Place on a greased or sprayed baking sheet. Make shallow cuts about 1½ inches around outside of the ring. Cover and let rise in a warm place until double in bulk. Brush top with beaten egg. Bake at 400° for 30-40 minutes until golden brown.

Note: Cover the bread with sesame seeds before baking to make a traditional St. Joseph's bread.

Italian White Bean Salad

2 cans (15 oz.) cannelloni (white beans)

½ cup olive oil

1 teaspoon basil

⅔ cup red onion, chopped

2 tablespoons wine vinegar

Combine all the ingredients and toss well. Cover and refrigerate for several hours before serving.

Pesto Sauce

2 cups fresh basil leaves, packed
4 cloves garlic
¼ cup grated Italian cheese
¼ cup pignoli nuts (pine nuts)
Dash of pepper
1 cup olive oil

Put all the ingredients in a blender or food processor. Add ½ cup olive oil. Blend on a low speed, stopping every few seconds to scrape the sides. When everything is evenly mixed, slowly add the remaining olive oil. Blend to a smooth consistency.

Note: Fresh parsley may be substituted for some of the basil. This will keep for several weeks in the refrigerator if you add a thin layer of oil over the top of the pesto.

Shrimp Sauce for Spaghetti

The Italians who settled along the Texas Gulf Coast found shrimp and other types of fish plentiful!

1 pound fresh shrimp
1 cup chopped onion
¼ teaspoon salt
¼ teaspoon pepper
⅛ teaspoon oregano
¼ cup olive oil
2 garlic cloves, minced
¾ cup green pepper, chopped
Spaghetti
¼ cup Romano or Parmesan cheese

Shell and devein the shrimp. Sauté the garlic, onion, green pepper, salt, pepper, and oregano in the oil until the onions are soft. Add the shrimp. Stir and cook over low heat for about 10 minutes until shrimp are pink and thoroughly heated. Cook the spaghetti until al dente; drain and toss gently with the shrimp mixture. Sprinkle with the cheese.

Palm Sunday Macaroni

This is a meatless dish that can be served on Palm Sunday as well as at other times.

1   pound ziti or other pasta
2   cans (8 oz.) tomato sauce
⅔   cup Italian seasoned bread crumbs
½   cup chopped pecans
½   cup Romano cheese

Cook the ziti until it is al dente. Drain. Stir in 1 cup tomato sauce. Add the bread crumbs, cheese, and pecans. Add the remaining tomato sauce, heat until warm, and serve.

Risotto Milanese
(Rice Milan Style)

1   cup finely chopped onion
4   tablespoons butter or margarine
2½ cups rice or risotto
¾   cup white wine
6-8 cups chicken broth
½   cup Parmesan cheese
1   tablespoon butter or margarine

In a large saucepan sauté the onion in 4 tablespoons butter. Add the rice, mixing well to completely coat the rice with butter. Add the wine. Continue heating and stirring until the wine has evaporated. Stir in enough broth to cover the rice. Stir occasionally, adding more broth so the rice won't scorch, until it is tender, 15-20 minutes. Stir in the cheese and the last tablespoon of butter.

Salsa per Pesce
(Sauce for Fish)

2 hard-boiled eggs
⅔ cup olive oil
4 anchovy fillets
½ teaspoon lemon juice

Put everything in a blender or food processor. Blend until the sauce has a creamy consistency. Heat, if desired. Serve over grilled or broiled fish.

Italian Baked Eggplant

2 eggplants, peeled and cut into 1½-inch slices
½ cup chopped celery
1 medium onion, chopped
1 clove garlic, minced
½ cup oil (divided use)
1 cup grated Romano cheese
½ pound ground beef
1 can (8 oz.) tomato sauce
1 can (6 oz.) tomato paste
3 cups water
½ teaspoon salt
¼ teaspoon pepper
2 tablespoons sugar

Put the sliced eggplant in a large bowl, cover with water, and add 1 teaspoon salt. Soak the eggplant to remove the bitterness while mixing the other ingredients. Sauté the onion, garlic, and celery in a small amount of the oil until tender. Add the tomato paste, tomato sauce, salt, pepper, and sugar. Add the water and simmer uncovered for about 30-40 minutes. Rinse the eggplant, drain, and dry with paper towels. Fry the eggplant in the remaining oil until tender and slightly brown. Brown the ground beef. In a casserole layer the eggplant, beef, cheese, and then sauce. Repeat layers, ending with cheese. Bake at 350° for 45 minutes. Serve hot!

Ring Cookies

⅓ cup shortening

1 beaten egg

2½ cups flour

⅔ cup sugar

⅓ cup milk

1 teaspoon baking powder

½ teaspoon vanilla

Mix all ingredients together. Roll into a ¼-inch thick rope. Cut into 3-inch lengths and shape into rings. Bake at 350° for nine minutes until lightly brown. Dip in icing.

Icing for Ring Cookies:

1¾ cups powdered sugar

2 tablespoons milk (more if needed)

½ teaspoon vanilla

Food coloring (optional)

Mix the sugar, milk, and vanilla until the consistency of thick gravy. Add food coloring, if desired. Frost by dumping all the cookies into the bowl of icing. Gently mix to cover the cookies with icing. Pour the iced cookies onto wax paper, separate, and let dry. Sprinkle with colored sugar while still sticky, if desired.

Note: Use almond or lemon flavoring in the cookies and icing for variety.

Lena Jackson gave me the following cookie recipes. She remembers helping her mother make them. Eating these cookies was always a wonderful treat!

Fig Cookies

Ground Fig Filling:

2   pounds figs

1   pound raisins

Orange zest from 2 navel oranges

2   cups water

1½ cups brown sugar

½   teaspoon allspice

½   teaspoon cloves

Boil together the water, sugar, and seasonings. Add figs, raisins, and orange zest. Lower heat and stir. When the liquid is absorbed, remove from heat. Cool. Chop in food processor. Add chopped nuts if desired.

Fig Cookie Pastry:

4   eggs

½   cup milk

1   cup vegetable oil

2   tablespoons vanilla

6   cups flour

3   tablespoons baking powder

1½ cups sugar

Mix dry ingredients together. Beat together the eggs, milk, oil, and vanilla. Slowly add the dry ingredients, mixing well between each addition. You will need to use your hands to work in the last of the flour. Knead lightly. Take a small amount of the dough and roll out into strips about 6 to 8 inches long and about 3 inches wide. Put a spoonful of filling in the center of each strip. Bring the dough together and overlap. Seal the dough with your fingers. Roll and cut into shapes. Bake at 400° for 20 to 25 minutes on a greased cookie sheet. Ice with cookie icing.

Pignolati

Dough:

- 6 eggs
- 4 cups flour
- 2 teaspoons baking powder

Oil for deep frying

Syrup:

- 1⅔ cups dark corn syrup
- ⅔ cup white sugar

Beat eggs with a mixer until foamy. Add flour and baking powder and knead until smooth. Let the dough rest for about an hour. Cut into small pieces and roll out like long spaghetti. Cut into ½-inch pieces and deep fry in oil until golden brown. Heat the sugar and syrup until it reaches 240°, the soft ball stage. Reduce heat to simmer and add about 5 cups of cooked dough, gently mixing to evenly coat the pieces. Add more cooked dough if needed to absorb all the syrup. Pour into a well-buttered pan and flatten. Let cool. Cut into squares and enjoy!

Aniseed Cookies

- ⅔ cup butter or margarine
- 4 eggs
- 1½ cups sugar
- 1 teaspoon vanilla
- 1 teaspoon almond flavoring
- 4 cups flour
- ½ teaspoon salt
- 2 teaspoons baking powder
- 4 teaspoons aniseed
- 1 cup blanched almonds, chopped

Cream the butter and sugar. Add eggs and flavorings. Mix well. Add remaining ingredients to make a soft dough. Take enough dough to make a 1½ inch "snake" as long as your cookie sheet. Place about 4 of these "snakes" on each pan. Bake at 325° for 30-35 minutes until slightly golden. Remove from the oven and slice each "snake" diagonally every ½ inch. Place sliced side down on the cookie sheet. Return to the oven to brown, about 10 minutes.

Scalidi

6   cups flour

1   cup (16 tablespoons or 2 sticks) butter, margarine, or shortening

5   eggs

1   cup sugar

2   teaspoons vanilla

1   teaspoon salt

4   teaspoons baking powder

Combine the dry ingredients. Cut in the butter or shortening. In a separate bowl, beat the eggs. Add the sugar and vanilla and beat well. Add the egg mixture to the flour mixture and blend. Let the dough rest for a few minutes. Roll dough into pieces 2 inches long and ½-inch thick. Deep fry each cookie in oil until golden brown. Drain and cool. Frost with the icing below:

Icing:

1   pound box of powdered sugar (about 3½ cups)

¼   cup (4 tablespoons) butter or margarine

Milk, as needed

Mix the sugar and butter well. Add just enough milk so the icing will spread easily.

Resources

Cookbooks

The African-American Kitchen, Angela Medearis, Dutton Books. 1994.

American Indian Cooking and Herb Lore, Cherokee Publications. 1973.

Buten Appetit!, Sophienburg Museum, New Braunfels, Texas. 1978.

Cookbook, compiled by the Sisterhood of Temple Rodef Sholom, Waco, Texas. 1966.

Danevang Community Cookbook, 1895-1985, Danevang Community. 1985.

Delectably Danish, Recipes and Reflections, Julie Jensen McDonald. 1982.

Golden Delights of Armstrong School, Armstrong Elementary School, Dallas, Texas.

The Jewish Cookbook, Pauline Frankel, Nitty Gritty Productions. 1971.

The Jewish Holiday Kitchen, Joan Nathan, Schocken Books. 1979.

Lone Star Legacy II, Austin Junior Forum. 1985.

The Melting Pot, The University of Texas Institute of Texan Cultures at San Antonio. 1997.

Our Favorite Cook Book, Texas Wendish Heritage Society, Serbin, Texas. 1975.

Preserving Our Italian Heritage, Sons of Italy. 1991.

Scots Lore and More, Highland Park High School, Dallas, Texas. 1992.

Southern Accent, Junior League of Pine Bluff, Arkansas. 1976.

Swedish Recipes, American Daughters of Sweden. 1955.

T'ai Bien, Women of St. George, Vicksburg, Mississippi. 1988.

Texas Rose of Tralee Cookbook. Texas Rose of Tralee Committee, Dallas, Texas. 1992.

Tex-Mex Cookbook, Jane Butel, Three Rivers Press. 1980.

Thunder in the Kitchen, Recipes and Memories, Thunder Alliance. n.d.

Ukrainian Christmas, Mary Ann Wolock Vaughn, Ukrainian Heritage Company. 1982.

West Heritage Cookbook, People of West, Texas. 1986.

Books

Davis, John L. *Texans One and All*, The University of Texas Institute of Texan Cultures at San Antonio. 1998.

Larsen, Jeanette Lucille. *Danevang, Texas—A History & Genealogy of the Danish Colony*. McDowell Publications, Utica, Kentucky. 1993.

Metcalfe, Edna. *The Trees of Christmas*, Abingdon Press, Nashville, TN. 1969.

Silverthorne, Elizabeth. *Christmas in Texas*, Texas A&M University Press, College Station, TX. 1990.

Tyler, Ron and Lawrence Murphy. *The Slave Narratives of Texas*, State House Press, Austin, TX. 1997.

Weiner, Hollace Ava. *Jewish Stars in Texas*, Texas A&M University Press, College Station, TX. 1999.

Online Sources:

The Handbook of Texas Online, http://www.tsha.utexas.edu/handbook/online/articles/view

African American Churches	Home Altars
African Americans	Irish
Apaches	Irish impresario John McMullen
Black Codes	Italians
Black Cowboys	Juneteenth
Caddos	Mariachi Music
Catholic Church	Mexican Americans
Cherokees	Native Americans
Comanches	Quinceañeras
Danes	Scots
Danevang, Texas	Slavery
Edna, Texas	Swedes
Fiestas Patrias	Swenson, Swante Magnus
Folk Drama	Syrian-Lebanese
Folk Festivals	Tex-Mex Foods
Free Blacks	Vaquero
Galveston Movement	

Jewish Weddings and Customs, http://ultimatewedding.com/custom/jewish.htm

Texas Historical Commission, http://www.thc.state.tx.us/Aabro.html

Juneteenth: Freedom Revisited, http://www.si.edu/organiza/museums/anacost/june.htm

Wendish Heritage, Concordia, University@Austin, http://www.concordia.edu/ethn.htm

A Shared Past—New Immigrants in Texas, http://riceinfo.rice.edu/armadillo/Texas/Sharedpast/newimmi.html

Juneteenth Celebrates African American Freedom, http://nando.atevo.com/guides/fotd/0%2C1310%2COO.html

African Weddings, http://www.melanet.com/awg/start.html

Polish Christmas, http://www.polstore.com/html/polishchristmas.html

Introduction from Polish Folk Costumes, http://chebucto.ns.ca/~aa051/pfc.intro.html

Dallas Morning News, "Make Your Own Dead Heads," Ellen Sweets, October 27, 1999.

   "Quinceañera Gives Families, Businesses Reason to Celebrate," August 11, 1999.

   "Day of the Dead Becoming Increasingly Commercialized." David McLemore, October 25, 1999.

   "The Forgotten Sacrifices of Tejanos in Texas' Fight." 1989.

San Antonio Express-News, "Polish Prime Minister Visits Panna Maria," Joseph Barrios, July 11, 1998.

Institute of Texas Cultures Vertical Files:
   "An Old World Christmas"
   "Sicilian-Texan Folklore Within the Context of the Feast of St. Joseph"
   "The Origin of the St. Joseph Altar"

City of Austin Library Vertical Files:
   "Fiesta del Diez y Seis"
   "A Czech Christmas"
   "Attire of Early Settlers Reflected Home Country"
   "Czech Heritage Week"
   "Czech Contributions to Texas Music"

Index to Recipes

217